TANKMASTER

A practical guide to choosing your

AQUARIUM
PLANTS

PETER HISCOCK

BARRON'S

Author

Peter Hiscock began keeping fish and aquariums as a child, inspired by his parents, both accomplished marine biologists. He was appointed manager of a retail aquatics outlet at just 17 years of age and went on to complete aquatic studies at Sparsholt College in Hampshire, UK. He entered publishing with contributions to the aquatic press. His main interests include fish behavior and the interaction of fish with their environment, as well as aquascaping and the natural habitats of aquarium species.

First edition for the United States and Canada published in 2001 by Barron's Educational Series, Inc.
First published in 2001 by Interpet Publishing
© Copyright 2001 by Interpet Publishing

All inquiries should be addressed to:
Barron's Educational Series, Inc.
250 Wireless Boulevard
Hauppauge, New York 11788
http://www.barronseduc.com

International Standard Book Number 0-7641-5356-0
Library of Congress Catalog Card Number 2001091844

Printed and Bound in Hong Kong
9 8 7 6 5 4 3 2 1

Below: In this planted aquarium a clump of Java moss links the background of Amazon swordplants to the lower-growing cryptocorynes featured at the front of the tank.

Contents

Here, a stunning red tiger lotus adds drama to an otherwise formal display.

Focus on plants

The aquatic environment is a dynamic, constantly changing one, and both plants and fish require certain conditions to thrive. To keep fish correctly, you must try to re-create an environment that is similar biologically, chemically, physically, and, ideally, aesthetically to their natural habitat. The same is true for plants; their biological needs include the correct lighting and a good nutrient supply, so that photosynthesis, growth, and reproduction can take place. Chemical needs demand that the water quality be suitable for plants to obtain nutrients and release wastes without hindering their growth through a buildup of pollutants or toxins. Physical needs can be related to a nutrient-rich substrate of a suitable texture in which plants can grow roots. If all the above are provided and correctly maintained, the plants provide the aesthetics themselves.

For new fishkeepers there are many hurdles to overcome and they need to acquire a certain amount of knowledge before they can become successful aquarists. Fortunately, if they look in the right places, there is also a great deal of information and advice available that will help them learn the basics quickly and steadily. On the other hand, aquarium plants are a different kettle of – plants. The conditions required for healthy plant growth are rarely found in a "standard" aquarium and conditions that are perfect for fish are not necessarily ideal for plants. The question "Why can't I keep plants?" could have many answers, because what you need to achieve is a combination of conditions that together allow plants to thrive in the aquarium. This book aims for a straightforward explanation of how to provide these conditions, with a detailed examination of water quality and filtration and how to provide lighting and substrates that will suit both fish and plants. Continuing care of your planted aquarium is important too, and sections on planning, feeding, planting, and propagation will help you to maintain a healthy and enviable display. A major part of the book is devoted to a detailed examination of a wide variety of generally available plants for each zone of the aquarium.

Every aquarist wants to keep healthy fish and it is worth remembering that in a fully planted and aquascaped environment, your fish will not only enjoy better health, but will also show brighter colors and behave more naturally. Most important, they will become just one aspect of a larger design.

Much like fish, plants require specific conditions to grow healthily and reproduce. These requirements usually have a physical basis and by examining the biology of plants, we can understand the conditions they need, why they need them, and the best methods of providing them.

Photosynthesis

Plants are unique in the way they obtain energy for growth by harnessing the power of light. Within the plant's cells there are chloroplasts, structures that contain the green pigment chlorophyll. Chlorophyll traps light energy and uses it to convert water and carbon dioxide (CO_2) into glucose and oxygen. In this process, water (H_2O) is split into hydrogen (H_2) and oxygen (O). The hydrogen then binds to carbon dioxide to form glucose, as shown at right.

Glucose Oxygen is released as a by-product of photosynthesis, but glucose is retained and used as a source of food. Because glucose is soluble, it must be quickly converted into an insoluble form – starch. If left in its soluble form, it would quickly absorb water through osmosis and enlarge the cells within the plant. However, starch is stored in the plant cells until needed, at which point it is converted back into glucose and transported around the plant. Glucose is a simple sugar and is used as a food source, needed in all living cells, for processes such as repair, growth, and reproduction.

The rate at which plants photosynthesize is governed by a number of environmental factors. For the best plant growth and health, it is important to

How photosynthesis works

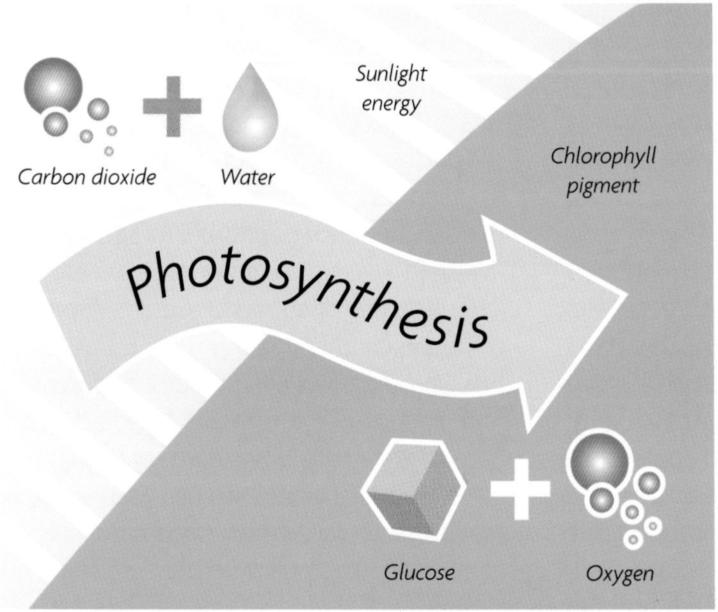

Carbon dioxide + Water

Sunlight energy

Chlorophyll pigment

Photosynthesis

Glucose + Oxygen

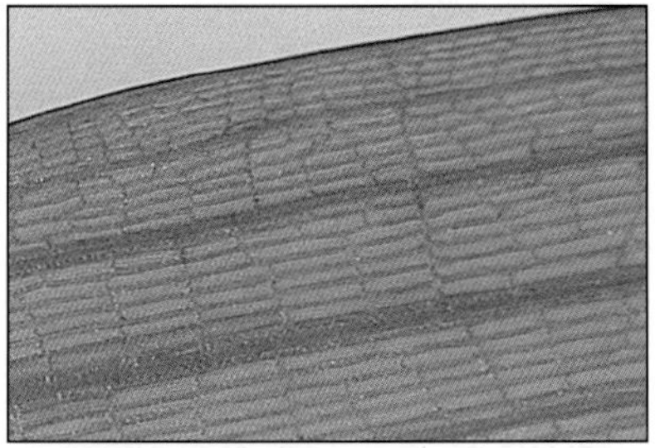

Right: This closeup view of an aquatic plant leaf clearly shows the "ribs" and "veins" that support the structure of the leaf and that are used to transport water, nutrients, and food products around the plant.

provide conditions that allow optimum levels of photosynthesis. The major influences on photosynthesis are the levels of light and CO_2 and the temperature of the surrounding environment. As with any biological process, it is the one limiting factor (the factor in shortest supply) that governs the rate of photosynthesis. Temperature rises generally increase rates of photosynthesis, providing they are within the plant's specific temperature tolerances. Within a plant's temperature tolerances, the rate of photosynthesis will double for every 10°C (18°F)

increase in temperature. If the temperature rises too high, the rate of photosynthesis will level off and eventually begin to drop.

Providing CO_2 levels are suitably high, the rate of photosynthesis in plants is directly proportional to the amount of light available. Until a light saturation point is reached, an increase in light intensity will result in an increase in photosynthesis. Conversely, providing light levels are sufficient, an increase in the amount of CO_2 available to the plants will increase their rate of photosynthesis.

To photosynthesize correctly, a plant must have a suitable amount of chlorophyll within its tissues. The formation of chlorophyll requires nitrogen (N) and mineral nutrients such as iron (Fe) and magnesium (Mg). (Iron is an important part of the enzymes that help to produce chlorophyll and magnesium lies at the center of the chlorophyll molecule.) To ensure that plants photosynthesize at an optimum rate, it is vital, therefore, to provide a suitably intense light, the correct temperature range, and abundant amounts of CO_2 and minerals, including iron.

Oxygen deficiency in planted aquariums

Plants produce more oxygen in a 24-hour period than they use up in respiration (see pages 10-11). This is why many plants that photosynthesize rapidly are sold as "oxygenating plants". However, an aquarium is an "enclosed environment," with a greater quantity of living organisms in relation to the volume of water than would be found in natural water bodies, such as lakes, rivers, and streams. At night, when plants stop producing oxygen and continue to respire, other organisms such as fish and bacteria also respire, and the combined effect can result in a dramatic decrease in oxygen levels. Aeration is the obvious solution, but plants do not appreciate high oxygen levels (see page 36), so oxygen levels soon become a problem. Use aeration only if the decrease in oxygen is adversely affecting the fish and use it at night only when necessary. In a heavily planted tank, check the livestock in the morning, just as light starts to reach the aquarium, for signs of oxygen deficiency, such as gasping at the surface or rapid breathing.

Limiting factors for photosynthesis

Providing the environment in terms of water quality and nutrients is adequate, there are three factors that affect the rate of photosynthesis.

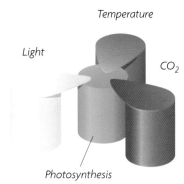

1 *Light, temperature, and carbon dioxide (CO_2) are limiting factors of photosynthesis. The rate is halted only by one or more of these factors.*

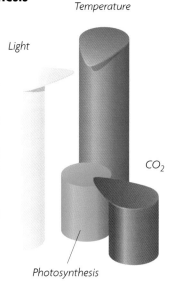

2 *In tanks without additional CO_2, an increase in light and/or temperature has no effect on photosynthesis rate. CO_2 is now the limiting factor.*

3 *Once additional supplies of CO_2 are added to the aquarium system, photosynthesis will increase toward a more optimal rate.*

Respiration

All living organisms respire in one form or another, and respiration takes place in all plant cells. The function of respiration is to break down food sources and release energy into the cell. Respiration uses up oxygen and releases carbon dioxide as a by-product, and is a process that continues day and night. The process of respiration is almost the opposite of photosynthesis, as can be seen below. Both photosynthesis and respiration take place during the day, but photosynthesis stops at night, while respiration continues. At night or during periods of darkness, plants will use up oxygen and release carbon dioxide. Because energy is used for

How respiration works

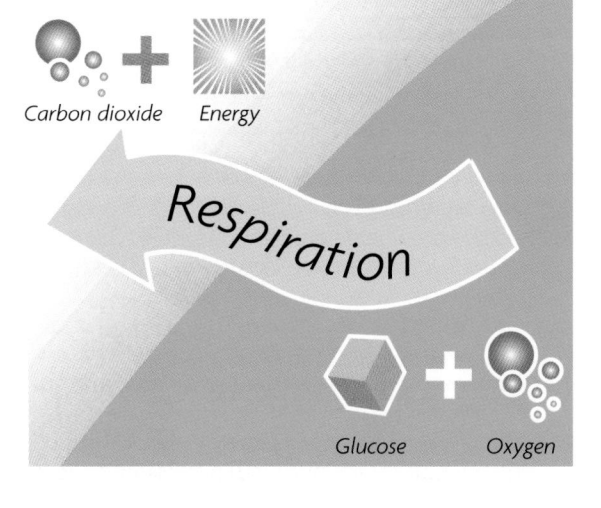

Carbon dioxide   Energy

Respiration

Glucose   Oxygen

The day-night cycle in the aquarium

Respiration and photosynthesis play an important part in oxygen and carbon dioxide levels in the aquarium. In a well-planted aquarium, significant fluctuations can occur within a 24-hour period.

■ Oxygen

■ Carbon dioxide

Fish respiration

Plant photosynthesis

Plant respiration

Fish respiration

Plant respiration

DAY *During the day, or in hours of artificial light, both plants and fish respire, using up oxygen and releasing carbon dioxide (CO_2). However, plants photosynthesize during the day, producing more oxygen and using up CO_2. In a healthy, well-planted aquarium the oxygen level is increased, while CO_2 is used up during the day.*

NIGHT *Photosynthesis stops at night, while respiration in both fish and plants continues. The result is that at night, oxygen levels are diminished, while CO_2 levels rise. In a well-planted aquarium, it is important to have adequate surface movement at night to allow for the release of CO_2 and to encourage the replenishment of oxygen.*

many processes in the plant, not just respiration, it is vital that the plant gains far more food from photosynthesis than it uses up in respiration. In an average 24-hour period, a plant will produce more oxygen and use up more carbon dioxide in photosynthesis than it will use oxygen and produce carbon dioxide during respiration.

Leaves and stems

Aquatic plants are perfectly designed for life underwater. Their stems and leaves have far less supporting tissue than terrestrial plants because they rely on the surrounding water for support. A system of air cavities, mainly in the stem, maintains the plants' buoyancy and this, combined with less rigid supporting tissue, allows the plants to be far more flexible underwater, bending and moving with the current.

The leaves of aquatic plants are also much thinner than those of terrestrial plants. This is mainly due to a very thin cuticle – the outermost protective layer that in terrestrial plants prevents them from drying out. A thinner, delicate leaf is more efficient at photosynthesis because light is able to penetrate the entire leaf. Even so, most chloroplast cells in the leaf are found near the surface, where the light is stronger. This is why the upper side of a leaf is often greener than the underside. A thin cuticle also allows aquatic plants to obtain nutrients and exchange gases directly between the leaf and the surrounding water.

Some plants obtain the bulk of their nutrients from the water and not the substrate. In this case, the roots are used simply as an anchor.

Inside a leaf and plant cell

As the section of vallisneria at right shows, aquatic plant leaves are very thin, allowing light to penetrate easily.

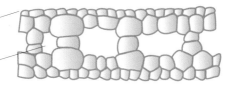

Thin cuticle layer on both surfaces of the leaf.

Air spaces provide support and structure.

The conversion of CO_2 into glucose takes place in this nutrient-rich liquid.

Inside each chloroplast, the green chlorophyll pigment is contained in plates that move toward the light like solar panels.

Liquid vacuole used for storage and water transport.

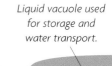

Respiration occurs in these cell structures called mitochondria.

The nucleus is the "control center" for each cell.

Cellulose cell walls made from strong polysaccharide matrix.

Right: *At the right temperature, with high CO_2, strong lighting, and a good nutrient supply, the rate of photosynthesis is optimized. Bubbles of oxygen are forming on this plant leaf as a result of photosynthesis.*

Left: *This cabomba is a true aquatic plant. Its thin leaves and stems are designed for buoyancy and flexibility under water. Out of water, it becomes limp and useless.*

Water quality and filtration

Water chemistry is possibly the most important aspect of fishkeeping, and the same applies to plantkeeping. Luckily, most plants are generally very versatile and able to adapt to a wide range of conditions. However, some delicate species are much more particular and if they are to do well, conditions in the aquarium must closely mimic those found in their natural habitat.

The two most important water quality factors for aquarium plants are hardness and pH, and we will look at these in detail.

Water hardness

Water is often termed "hard" or "soft," especially in relation to keeping certain fish species. Some fish, such as discus or tetras, prefer soft water, while others, such as African lake cichlids, are more at home in hard water.

Water hardness is a measure of the amount of dissolved minerals, principally calcium and magnesium salts, in the water. Water rich in calcium salts is "hard," while water with few dissolved salts is "soft." Total hardness is made up of carbonate (temporary) and permanent hardness and is measured in degrees of hardness (°dGH). Carbonate hardness (measured in °dH) is caused by the presence of calcium bicarbonate and can be removed by boiling water. Permanent hardness is caused by calcium sulphate and cannot easily be removed.

In their natural environments, plants live in a wide range of hardness levels, although most are found in soft water. For plant growth, carbonate hardness is the most important factor and should be kept at

Above: Xiphophorus maculatus *(the platy), shown here against cabomba, prefers slightly alkaline conditions, which may not suit all plant species.*

Right: Many delicate fish species, such as these discus (Symphysodon sp.) will thrive in the same conditions as aquarium plants.

Levels of water hardness

0-5°dGH	Very soft
6-9°dGH	Soft
10-14°dGH	Medium
15-19°dGH	Medium hard
20-28°dGH	Hard
Over 28°dGH	Very hard

Biogenic decalcification

When CO_2 is in short supply, some plants perform a process called biogenic decalcification to obtain CO_2 from calcium bicarbonate $Ca(HCO_3)_2$. This process requires a large amount of energy, so it is only used as an emergency measure. The effect can be seen as a white chalk deposit on the undersides of plant leaves. If this occurs in a well-planted aquarium, the release of carbonates can drastically raise pH levels, causing the water to become rapidly alkaline. Such a quick change in pH is very harmful to any fish in the tank.

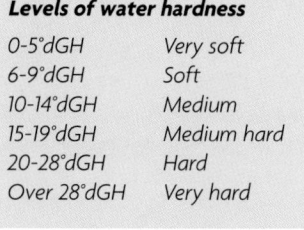

medium-soft levels. Fertilization with CO_2 should be enough to keep carbonate hardness at a low level. Ideally, total hardness should be maintained at around 8-15°dGH and carbonate hardness at 4-10°dH.

Acidity/alkalinity (pH)

The pH reading of water reflects how alkaline or acidic it is. Water is made up of positively charged hydrogen ions (H+) and negatively charged hydroxyl ions (OH-). The pH level is a measure of the ratio of these two ions in a body of water. Acidic water has more hydrogen ions, while alkaline water contains more hydroxyl ions. Neutral water contains an equal ratio. The pH scale runs from 1 to 14, with 7 being neutral. (Each step of one unit on the scale represents a ten-fold change in pH level.) Anything below 7 is acidic and above 7 is alkaline. Aquarium fish generally live in water with a pH of between 5 and 9; very few fish will survive happily in water with a pH level outside this range. Some fish, such as discus or dwarf cichlids, prefer acid, or low pH, conditions. Others, such as the Rift Lake cichlids, prefer alkaline, or high pH, conditions.

In nature, plants can be found almost wherever there are fish, although they have a lower tolerance to extreme pH levels. Most prefer a pH level between 6 and 7.5; however, some will adapt to harder water.

The pH reading is closely linked to levels of carbon dioxide in the aquarium, because carbon dioxide produces carbonic acid, which is acidic and lowers pH. In planted aquariums, the pH level can fluctuate through a 24-hour period because plants produce CO_2 at night (which lowers pH), and consume CO_2 during the day by photosynthesis (which raises pH). Many fish will cope quite happily with this change, as the same fluctuations can happen in nature.

The pH level in most aquariums will drop over

Buffering capacity

Buffering capacity describes the ability of a body of water to maintain a stable pH level, or more accurately, to prevent drops in pH levels. Water contains buffers, often in the form of carbonates, that resist fluctuations in hydrogen ions, thereby reducing any severe drops in pH. Buffering capacity is closely linked to water hardness, and the same substances are involved in both processes; hard water is generally better buffered and has a higher alkalinity (pH) than soft water. The buffering capacity of water can be kept stable by routine water changes. It is vital to measure carbonate hardness regularly in planted aquariums, as the use of CO_2 can reduce the aquarium's buffering capacity and/or hardness. If all the available carbonates are used up, a severe drop in pH may result, which will be harmful to any fish in the aquarium. Plants are also affected by changes in pH, but not as drastically as fish. Most aquarium plants prefer a pH value of 6-7.5.

Carbonates are used up by acids in the aquarium.

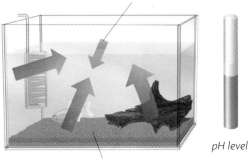

Carbonic, organic, and humic acids are continually produced.

Above: *A lack of water changes or using water with low hardness levels (such as R.O. water) without an artificial buffer will reduce carbonate levels. pH fluctuations may occur.*

Carbonates will "use up" acids in the aquarium.

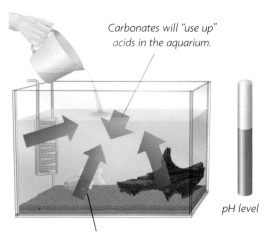

pH level

Acids are produced from CO_2, organics, and bogwood.

Above: *Regular water changes help to replenish carbonates, maintaining a good buffering capacity. In a well-buffered aquarium, the pH level will stay relatively constant.*

With no carbonates, there is no buffering capacity.

pH level

Acids will now affect the pH level.

Above: *With no carbonates and/or buffering capacity, any acids produced will lower the pH level. This can happen quickly, causing death to fish and damage to plants.*

time as a result of acids produced by waste organic matter, respiration, and filtration processes. Regular removal of waste matter and regular water changes will reduce this effect. pH changes are damaging to fish and plants only if they happen suddenly. Typical sudden changes may occur via water changes (the difference in pH between the new water and the aquarium water), algal blooms, or a reduction in the water's buffering capacity (see page 13).

Aquarium filtration

Filtration in aquariums is primarily designed to remove and break down waste toxins, which are damaging to fish, thus creating an environment suitable for fish to live in. In nature, this process is carried out by natural bacteria and organisms living within substrates and the

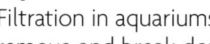

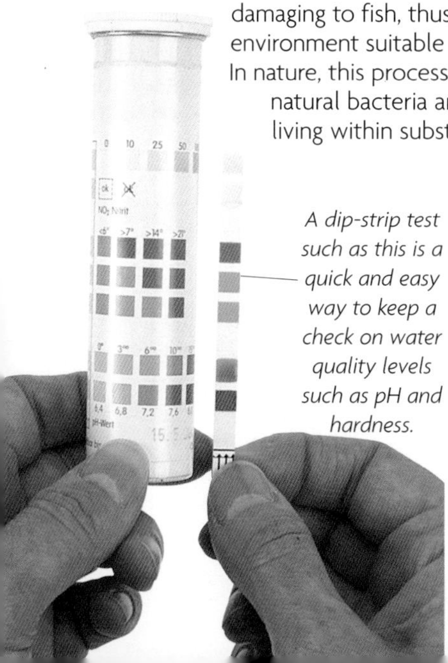

A dip-strip test such as this is a quick and easy way to keep a check on water quality levels such as pH and hardness.

Right: There are many reasons why algae may form in the aquarium and a small amount is natural. However, algal blooms such as this indicate that there is something wrong with the aquarium environment. (See page 46 for methods of preventing the buildup of algae.)

Filamentous algae such as this can quickly swamp plants and ruin a display.

Testing for hardness and pH

You can easily test your aquarium water for total hardness, carbonate hardness, and pH levels by using a brand name test kit. Test kits are available in three forms: liquid, tablet, and dip-strip. Each type has its own advantages and disadvantages, although dip-strip tests are by far the easiest to use. Multiple strips are available that provide readings for total hardness, carbonate hardness, and pH in one test.

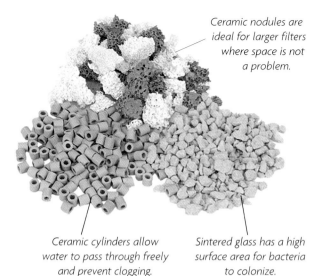

Ceramic nodules are ideal for larger filters where space is not a problem.

Ceramic cylinders allow water to pass through freely and prevent clogging.

Sintered glass has a high surface area for bacteria to colonize.

water body. In the aquarium, there are many more fish and plants compared to the available water volume, so the amount of these bacteria has to be artificially increased if they are to "clean" the water adequately. This is the function of filtration and it is required in one form or another in all aquariums. There are three main forms of filtration: mechanical, biological, and chemical.

Mechanical filtration

Mechanical filtration is simply the removal of any visible particles in the water. Fish do not especially mind if the water looks slightly dirty; in fact, this would probably be more like their natural habitats. For plants, however, suspended debris in the aquarium can block light, hindering photosynthesis and, in the case of fine-leaved plants, clogging the leaf structure. Mechanical filtration simply involves straining the water through a medium such as foam to trap any suspended particles.

Mechanical filter medium is available in various grades (coarse, medium, or fine) to trap different-sized particles. Filter floss is often used as a final "polishing" medium to remove the smallest particles from the water. Regular removal of wastes by methods such as gravel cleaning can also be regarded as mechanical filtration.

Biological filtration

Biological filtration is the most important filtration process and involves the breakdown and removal of organic pollutants, such as ammonia and nitrites, by bacteria. Most toxic organic pollutants cannot be visibly detected in the water, so without adequate biological filtration, your water could be crystal clear yet deadly. A biological filter medium is one with a high surface area on which bacteria can settle and remove pollutants by a process of oxidation. The media used for mechanical filtration, such as foams, often double as a biological medium. For larger filters and external filters, specially designed biological media are available, such as sintered glass or ceramic nodules, which have a much increased surface area that provides more efficient and balanced biological aquarium filtration.

Remember

Green water is caused by single-celled algae (see page 46) that may not be removed by mechanical filtration.

Chemical filtration

Chemical filtration removes pollutants such as metals and unwanted chemicals, which can enter the aquarium, and aids the removal of organic pollutants. Basically, chemical filtration is any form of filtration that alters the water's properties by removing one or more substances, and includes water softeners and even dechlorinators. Some chemical media, such as activated carbon, have a limited lifespan. If they are left in the aquarium too long, they will reach a point where they cannot contain any more pollutants and may even release them back into the water. Most chemical media need be used only when necessary and are not a vital part of filtration. In case of an unexpected water quality problem or the breakdown of biological filtration, chemical filtration can be used to remove pollutants quickly. In planted aquariums, avoid chemical filtration media, such as carbon, that remove a wide range of chemicals. This type of filtration may also remove many nutrients from the water, hindering plant growth. Many filters are supplied with activated carbon. If used in a planted aquarium, it is a good idea to remove the carbon and replace it with additional mechanical or biological filtration.

Certain aquarium plants, such as Aponogeton madagascariensis, *have a fine leaf structure. Good mechanical filtration will provide clear water and prevent the leaves from becoming clogged.*

Types of filter

The three most commonly available types of filtration are internal, external, and undergravel. In a planted aquarium, use only internal or external filtration. Undergravel filtration works by drawing water down through the substrate and back into the aquarium at the surface. The substrate acts as a mechanical and biological medium in which bacteria live.

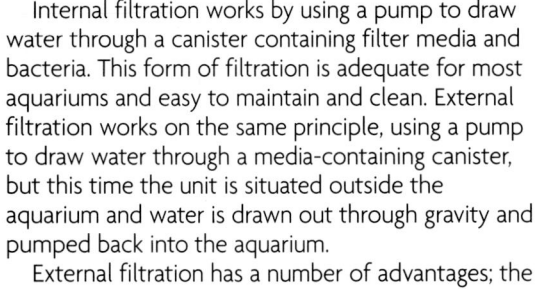

However, plants do not appreciate the flow of water through the substrate, as it disrupts and removes essential nutrients that the roots would normally absorb. Drawing water through the substrate also causes problems when using fine, nutrient-rich substrates that would be removed and scattered throughout the aquarium, causing the water to become dirty. Undergravel filtration in freshwater aquariums has largely been surpassed by the use of internal power filters.

Left: Internal filters are ideal for smaller aquariums. Compact and easy to use, they provide mechanical and biological filtration, and some, such as this one, also provide compartments for chemical filtration, if desired.

Internal filtration works by using a pump to draw water through a canister containing filter media and bacteria. This form of filtration is adequate for most aquariums and easy to maintain and clean. External filtration works on the same principle, using a pump to draw water through a media-containing canister, but this time the unit is situated outside the aquarium and water is drawn out through gravity and pumped back into the aquarium.

External filtration has a number of advantages; the fact that the unit is outside the aquarium allows the canister to be much larger and contain more filter media, thus increasing efficiency. As more space is available, additional media can be used for specific purposes, allowing the filter to become tailor-made to the aquarium.

Filtration for planted aquariums

Most filters are designed primarily to make the environment hospitable for fish, and provide little additional benefit for plants. When choosing a filtration system for a planted aquarium, there are a few points to consider. First, plants do not appreciate excess oxygen, so reduce aeration via surface movement from the filter pump. This can be done in two ways. First, make sure the filter turns over the volume of water in the aquarium once every hour. Allowing for media, pipework, and other obstructions, a 300-liter (66-gallon) aquarium should have a filter capable of moving about 370 liters per hour (81 gallons per hour). This is roughly half the rate normally recommended for aquariums. Second, position the outlet of the filter at least

Above: External filters are by far the best form of domestic filtration. As there is very little equipment inside the aquarium, there is more space for aquascaping. In addition, the external canister has a large volume, allowing more media to be used and thereby providing better filtration.

Anaerobic filtration

Bacteria that form in the aquarium filter are responsible for the breakdown of wastes, making the water safe for your fish to live in. Under normal (aerobic) conditions where oxygen is available, bacteria convert ammonia into nitrite and nitrite into nitrate, using up oxygen during the process. Aerobic filtration will remove ammonia and nitrite, while producing a gradual buildup of less toxic nitrates, which can be controlled through chemical filtration and regular water changes. If oxygen levels in the filter are reduced, conditions can become anaerobic and bacteria have to find a new source of oxygen. In these conditions, bacteria will, in a number of stages, convert nitrate into nitrogen gas, which is then released into the atmosphere. If managed correctly, a combination of aerobic and anaerobic filtration can effectively remove ammonia and nitrite, while also lowering nitrate levels.

Right: Allowing half of the sponge media in a filter to clog will allow both aerobic and anaerobic filtration, increasing the effectiveness of the filter and reducing ammonia, nitrites, and nitrates.

5-10 cm (2-4 in) below the water surface, again to reduce surface movement. A reduced flow rate through the filter also increases the likelihood of anaerobic bacteria developing, which helps to reduce nitrates. Nitrate levels are particularly important in the planted aquarium. Whereas fish will tolerate reasonably high levels of nitrates, plants do not appreciate levels above 30-40 mg/liter. Plants do use nitrates as a food source, although in natural conditions, nitrates rarely rise above 1-2 mg/liter.

Check the flow regularly to ensure that the filter is not becoming too blocked up. When it is time to clean the sponges, clean only one, leaving the other to become clogged.

Anaerobic conditions in clogged patches contain bacteria that reduce nitrates.

Obstructed media force oxygenated water to travel through a set path.

This sponge is relatively clean, and aerobic bacteria here will reduce toxic ammonia and nitrites.

Anaerobic conditions will occur naturally in the deeper parts of the substrate, but to concentrate the process, they can be encouraged inside the filter. A slower flow rate will help to reduce the influx of oxygen to the filter, but to produce truly anaerobic conditions, you must prevent any replenishment of oxygen. This can be done by allowing part of the filter to clog. If half the filter sponge is left to clog, tracking will occur, which means that the flow of water will travel quickly through a limited number of paths, leaving patches of sponge with virtually zero flow, and anaerobic conditions. Allow only half the sponge to clog, as aerobic action is still needed to remove ammonia. Encouraging anaerobic filtration in the aquarium provides an effective method of reducing nitrates without using chemical media, which can remove useful nutrients.

Below: During routine maintenance, clean only half the filter sponge at one time. Simply squeeze most of the dirt out in a bowl of water taken from the aquarium. Use a new bowl and keep this for aquarium use only.

Using the right substrate

One of the main reasons for continued lack of success with aquarium plants is a biologically inactive substrate. A substrate of clean, medium- / large-grade inert gravel offers nothing more than an anchor to hold plants in place. The ease with which water flows through this kind of substrate will remove nutrients, create oxygen-rich conditions, and cool plant roots, all of which will severely hinder plant growth. A planted aquarium should have a mixture of substrates, all of which play a part in providing the best overall conditions for growth.

The function of substrate

Substrate has many functions in the aquarium. It provides a suitable medium for holding plants and decor in place and creates an aesthetically pleasing aquarium, but for plants and their development, a good substrate will provide much more. Most plants obtain the bulk of their nutrients through their roots. In the aquarium, the substrate must provide a constant and easily available supply of nutrients directly to the root system.

To provide enough depth for root growth, the substrate in a planted aquarium should be 5-7.5 cm (2-3 in) deep. In this section we examine different substrates and their role in the planted aquarium.

Pea gravel

The standard aquarium gravel, also called pea gravel due to its rounded, smooth appearance, is available in a number of grades from 2 mm up to 10 mm (0.08-0.4 in). Although often described as inert, it is very rarely completely inert and contains small amounts of calcium and/or lime. Small-grade pea gravel will provide good support and is a reasonably efficient rooting medium, but beyond this, pea gravel offers little for the plants. It can be used as the main substrate in combination with nutrient-rich substrates or clay-based materials. Ideally, pea gravel should be used only as a top-layer medium, holding plants and decor in place and providing an aesthetically pleasing substrate. Alternatively, lime-free gravel will do the same job, but with more benefits for plant life.

Lime-free substrates

Quite simply put, lime-free gravel contains no lime, calcium, or other materials that may adversely affect plants and water quality. Most gravel substrates, including pea gravel, are made from a mixture of rock types so calcium-based rocks usually find their way into them. However, lime-free gravel is made up of completely inert quartz material and nothing else.

The range of substrates

Silver sand can be used as a base to support a heating cable.

Iron- and nutrient-rich laterite media will provide a layer of slow-release nutrients for plant roots.

Lime-free gravel can make up the bulk of the substrate and is a good, inert rooting medium.

The uppermost layer can be topped with pea gravel or a larger substrate. This layer is more aesthetic than functional.

Lime-free gravel is usually only available in small 2-3 mm (0.08-0.125 in) grade and makes an ideal rooting and supportive planting substrate. In a basic planted aquarium, lime-free gravel can be used as the sole substrate, but for more advanced aquariums or to promote better plant growth, it should be used in combination with other substrates.

Sand

As an alternative to gravel, sand can look very attractive in the aquarium, but problems arise if it is used as the sole substrate. Over time, sand will compact and create anaerobic conditions. The plants will not be adversely affected by this, but due to the small grain size of sand, water circulation will be reduced and stopped. A lack of circulation will cause the sand to become stagnant in anaerobic areas, resulting in the release of small quantities of noxious gases and causing the sand to turn black. You can prevent stagnation by regularly stirring the substrate, although plants and plant roots will not appreciate

this. However, sand does have an important role in the planted aquarium in conjunction with the use of heating cables and nutrient circulation, and we will look at this later.

Clay-based substrates

Clay-based substrates, usually called laterite, are rich in iron and release nutrients over a long period of time. When combined with acids in the water and also acids produced by plant roots, these nutrients become easily available for use.

Laterite is often reddish in color and usually available as a very fine, almost powdery medium. It is designed to be used together with a supportive substrate, such as pea gravel or lime-free gravel, and can be mixed with the lower two-thirds of the substrate or "sandwiched" between layers of substrates. If used in bulk, it can compact heavily, stopping nutrient flow and oxygen transfer. A mixture of lime-free quartz gravel and laterite makes a good basic substrate for plant growth.

Nutrient-rich substrates

Specially designed substrates are available that contain a multitude of nutrients and trace elements vital to plant health (see page 35). Most of these are soil-like in appearance and must be "sandwiched" between two fine-grade substrates that hold the nutrient-rich medium in place. If allowed to escape, some of the "soil" may float and muddy the water. You need only a thin spread of this substrate to provide significant benefits for the plants. Nutrient-rich substrates are artificially created and usually sold under a brand name. Ask your dealer for advice.

Unsuitable substrates

Choosing a suitable substrate is important, but possibly even more important is avoiding an unsuitable substrate, of which there are many. Larger substrates, such as gravel over 6 mm (0.25 in), will not provide a suitable rooting medium for plants. In addition, they allow too much water and oxygen to pass through the substrate, thus removing nutrients in the process. However, as long as it is inert, a large-grade substrate can be used as a thin top layer, purely for aesthetic purposes.

Any substrate that alters the water quality is also unsuitable. Most substrates in this category raise hardness and pH, which can result in a lower number of available acids to bind with useful nutrients. Typical examples are coral-based gravels, which are rich in calcium and designed for marine aquariums.

Peat is another unsuitable substrate occasionally recommended for planted aquariums. Although it is rich in nutrients, these are released quickly rather than slowly. An influx of too many nutrients will cause rapid algal growth, swamping plants and hindering their growth. Specifically designed nutrient-rich substrates or clay-based laterite

Left: Sand can be used as the sole substrate, but if it is not regularly disturbed it may compact and create dense anaerobic areas that release toxic gases and adversely affect plant roots. If possible, always use a combination of substrate materials.

substrates release nutrients slowly over longer periods of time, allowing plants to use up any available nutrients and eliminating the chance of "overloading" the system.

Do not use any terrestrial planting substrates in the aquarium, such as compost or potting soil. They are not designed for aquarium use and will release dangerous compounds into the water.

Above: *Washing substrate before use can take some time, but it is important to ensure that any dust and debris are removed; otherwise the aquarium water will become cloudy. Rinse the substrate until the water runs clear.*

Preparing and installing the substrate

Once an aquarium is running and fully stocked, it becomes a major overhaul to replace or change the substrate, so it is not only vital to choose the right substrate mixture, but also to install it correctly from the start. Preparing and placing the substrate in the tank can be one of the most time-consuming aquascaping activities, but it must be done properly.

All gravel substrates should be thoroughly washed to remove any dust and debris. Clean the substrate in small amounts under tapwater until the water runs clear. There is no need to clean sand, as it contains minimal dust, and cleaning will prove tricky at best.

The substrate should be 5-7.5 cm (2-3 in) deep to provide ample room for rooting. Rocks and decor can be used to create raised areas of substrate toward the rear of the aquarium. This effect looks particularly good when low-growing foreground plants are used in front of the raised area. If you are using a nutrient-rich layer, sandwich it between two layers of substrate. Even with the best prewashing of substrate, you may find that the aquarium water will cloud slightly, but it should clear within 24 hours.

Substrate heating

In the streams and shallow riverbanks where many aquarium plants are naturally found, the uppermost layer of the substrate is often warmer than the surrounding water because it absorbs heat from the sun. The difference in temperature between the river or stream and the riverbed, combined with the action of underground springs, causes a constant movement of water through the substrate. Water

currents help to move nutrients around the substrate, making them easily available to plant roots. A substrate that is warmer than the surrounding water body creates its own currents of water movement through the transfer of heat, and these are called convection currents. Consequently, aquarium plants prefer to have a warmer substrate around their roots, and this can be achieved by gently heating the aquarium substrate by means of a heating cable.

A heating cable consists of a long cable trailed just above the glass bottom of the aquarium, underneath the substrate. The heat required to produce suitable convection currents is very little, so most heating cables are very low wattage and, although left on 24 hours a day, should not affect the water temperature of the tank to any great degree. The space directly around the heating cable should be able to absorb and distribute the heat quickly and evenly. This is where sand plays a part in the substrate. A 5-cm (2-in) layer of sand will hold the cable in place and allow heat to be spread around the cable beneath the main substrates. The slow convection currents will also carry small quantities of oxygen through the substrate, which prevents the sand from becoming stagnant.

Maintaining the substrate

Once the substrate is in place it will require little maintenance and should be left as it is to avoid disturbing the plant roots. Over time, organic wastes from fish and plants will collect in the top layers of the substrate. If this mulm is left, it will compact, use

Installing a heater cable and substrates

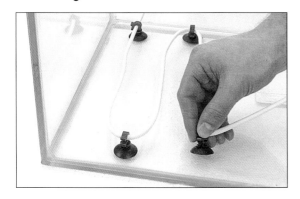

1 Attach the substrate heating cable to the base of the tank with suction cups. Depending on the cable wattage, leave a 5-10 cm (2-4 in) space between the loops of winding cable.

2 Add a layer of silver sand about 5 cm (2 in) deep. It should cover the cable by at least 1-2 cm (0.4-0.8 in). The silver sand helps to distribute heat from the cable quickly and evenly.

3 Place a thin layer of nutrient-rich substrate on top of the sand. This is an iron-rich laterite substrate, but there are other alternatives.

4 Finally, add a 5-10-cm (2-4-in)-deep layer of lime-free substrate. This quartz substrate is a good, inert rooting medium. Level the top.

5 The layers of substrate can be clearly seen here. If you wish, you can add a further decorative top layer purely for aesthetic purposes.

up oxygen, and release toxic hydrogen sulphide. To avoid this, the uppermost layer of the substrate should be regularly siphoned to reduce a buildup of waste material. This can be done at the same time as a water change, carrying out two jobs at once.

Any fine substrates (less than 2 mm/0.08 in) will compact over time, reducing water flow, allowing toxic gases to build up, and damaging roots. Check the substrate every few months by pushing a finger down to the base of the aquarium; there should not be a great deal of resistance. If compaction has occurred, use your fingers to disturb and loosen the substrate gently.

If the substrate or plant roots start turning black, it is highly likely that the substrate is becoming stagnant and anaerobic. Gas bubbles produced when the substrate is disturbed are also a sign of stagnation. This often happens if the substrate is old or not maintained properly. In this instance, gently disturb the substrate and a few hours later siphon off any mulm from the substrate surface. Providing the substrate is maintained properly (see page 43) and replaced at least every three years, stagnation or compaction should not be a problem.

In time, the nutrient-containing elements of the substrate will be exhausted and become ineffective, in which case they may need replacing. Most nutrient-rich substrates continue to release nutrients slowly for up to three years and can be left for this period without being changed. Replace the substrate after three years only if the plants are showing adverse signs. Established plants may find enough nutrients even when the nutrient release from the substrate is diminished. Removing and replacing the substrate can damage well-established plants; take care to minimize any detrimental effects. Follow the guidelines for moving established plants on page 42.

Choosing and planting

Once you have prepared a rough planting plan (see page 50), you should have a good idea of the species and quantities of each plant you require, which will make buying them a lot easier. The next stage is to buy the plants. It is possible to select and buy plants through mail order and the quality is usually reasonably high, but it is often better to choose your own stock from a good retailer, because this way you know exactly what you are getting. Find out when your retailer receives plant deliveries and obtain your plants on that day, when there is more variety available and the quality is often better.

Good-quality plants are easy to spot; they should have strong, vibrant colors (with the exception of some cryptocorynes, which are often naturally brown and subdued) and in most species, new growth should be visible. It is quite common for a perfectly healthy plant to have one or two brown or dying leaves, especially

toward the base of the plant, so there is no need to be overly fussy when choosing.

When you have chosen your plants, make sure they are packaged in a way that will avoid crushing. Bags filled with air provide cushioning. If the bags are tied or sealed, the plants will not require additional water and can be kept in the bags for a few hours without any adverse effects. Once you have bought the plants, remove any dead or dying leaves before planting.

Separating *Vallisneria spiralis*

1 Many bunched plants are supplied with a lead weight attached to the base. This should be removed before you put the plants in the aquarium; otherwise it may damage the roots and/or restrict the plant's growth.

2 Removing the lead weight from this vallisneria produces five individual plants, each with healthy roots. Plant them separately, leaving space between them to allow for growth.

Preparing for planting

Plants are supplied either potted or in bunches. Bunched plants are often held in place by a lead weight, which should be removed. You may then find that each bunch consists of a number of individual plants, and you should plant these separately. Plants with plenty of root growth, such as *Cryptocoryne* or *Echinodorus* species, may need to be trimmed. Cut the excess roots with a pair of sharp scissors, leaving them at least 2 cm (0.8 in) long. Even if the roots are healthy, they will sustain less damage when planted if you cut them straight across than if you try pushing long roots into the substrate.

Unfortunately, many bunched plants will have little or no root growth, because they are often simply cuttings taken from the tops of plants. However, if they are healthy, they should develop roots once they are planted in the substrate.

Potted plants are usually wrapped in a planting medium called rock wool, which is quite easy to remove and should be taken off. If the roots are firmly embedded in the rock wool, leave it on to avoid damaging the plant.

Before placing any plants in the aquarium, check each one thoroughly for snails. Most aquarium plants are now grown in virtually snail-free environments, and good retailers will do their best to avoid introducing them, but a few will inevitably get through. It is possible to "dip" aquarium plants in a brand name chemical before introducing them into the aquarium to kill any snails. Unfortunately, many chemical snail killers will be ineffective against the eggs, so it is important to check for snail eggs (a small, jellylike substance) on plant leaves and stems.

When to fertilize new plants

Moving and introducing plants is stressful and damaging, and at first they will need to expend energy on producing new roots and becoming established. The nutrients provided by fertilization are used in the greatest quantities when the plants are healthy and growing (already established), so plants are unlikely to need many nutrients during the first week or two. For this reason, fertilization (apart from the introduction of CO_2) should be avoided during the first week, and given at a reduced rate in the second week. If the aquarium is over-fertilized, algae will quickly grow and become a significant problem.

Separating *Ludwigia palustris*

1 Ludwigia palustris is a common, attractive, and versatile aquarium plant usually sold as cuttings embedded in rock wool with a little root growth. The plant, with rock wool, should slide easily out of the pot.

2 Once the plant is removed, carefully unravel the rock wool. You may find that there are as many as three separate pieces of rock wool, each containing two or three individual plants.

3 If there are developed roots embedded in the rock wool, leave the plants grouped in the wool. For the best effect in the aquarium, place the separate groups close to one another.

23

Choosing and planting

Planting

The best planting method is to create a small dip in the substrate and push the plant into it. Then surround the plant with substrate, in much the same way as you would put garden plants in the soil. Be sure to leave sufficient space between the plants; otherwise light may be blocked out and the lower leaves of each plant will drop off. Plants that produce runners, spread, or develop to occupy large spaces also require sufficient space to grow into. You may find that a couple of days after you put them in, a few plants, especially ones that were originally bunched, will uproot themselves and float to the surface of the tank. If this happens, replant them.

Below: Position the rocks and bogwood before adding any plants to the aquarium. This will help to mark out the areas available for planting. Use contrasting plants with differing colors or leaf shapes for added impact.

Planting *Ludwigia palustris*

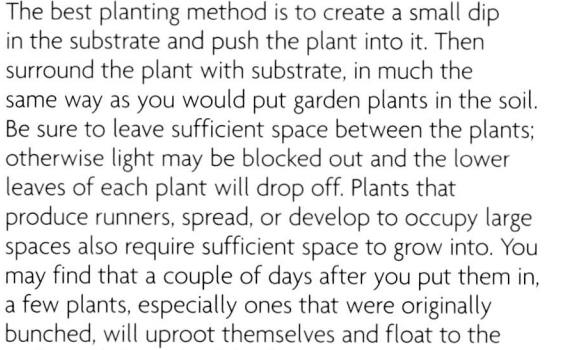

1 Supporting the plant lightly, use your fingers to create a dip in the substrate and hold it open. Disturb the substrate as little as possible.

2 Place the roots, still embedded in rock wool, into the substrate. Push the plant down until the top of the rock wool is just below the surface.

3 Use the remaining substrate to cover the surface of the roots and compact around the base, as you would with a terrestrial plant.

4 To create a more attractive display, place the same plants close together. Here they are put in 2.5-5 cm (1-2 in) apart. Alternatively, leave just enough room so that the tips of leaves on separate plants just touch.

Just as some terrestrial plants grow on trees, rocks, and other objects, rather than in soil, many aquatic plants have found it useful to grow on objects other than substrate. Java fern (*Microsorium pteropus*), Java moss (*Vesicularia dubyana*), African fern (*Bolbitis heudelotii*), and *Anubias* sp. have developed special roots that are able to attach to and grow securely in and on wood and porous rocks. Their preference to be planted on objects rather than in the substrate gives the aquarist a number of aquascaping opportunities without having to worry about the quality of substrate. Many of these "object-rooting" species will also grow, at least partially, out of water and can be raised to the upper reaches of the aquarium and allowed to grow through the surface.

Tying Java fern to bogwood

Left: This recently positioned Java fern should soon grow new roots and begin to spread across the length of the wood. If there is room on the bogwood, you can add other plants, such as dwarf anubias and Java moss.

1 *Removing rock wool from Java fern can be tricky, as the roots are often dense and tangled and damage is inevitable. However, with a little care and patience, any damage can be limited.*

2 *Trim any excess root with a pair of sharp scissors, leaving only 1-2 cm (0.4-0.8 in). This helps to minimize damage and encourages regrowth. Take care not to damage or cut the rhizome (the main root).*

3 *Tie the root firmly to the bogwood with black thread, which will be hardly noticeable and soon covered by new roots.*

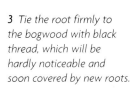

All plants need sufficient light to photosynthesize properly. In nature, this comes from sunlight, but in the confined conditions of the aquarium, you cannot rely on strong sunlight, as it is irregular and causes temperature fluctuations, as well as excessive algal growth. Furthermore, most aquarium plants come from tropical regions where day length varies little throughout the year, so the variations in sunlight and day length encountered in nontropical areas do not suit them. Instead, light has to be reproduced accurately to mimic the levels of light that the plants would receive in their natural environments.

Correct lighting is an area where many standard aquariums fall short of what is required, making it difficult to maintain aquarium plants successfully. Although lighting requirements do vary with individual species, most plants require more light than can be provided by a single fluorescent tube. To provide the correct light source in the aquarium we should look at the quality and characteristics of light required by aquarium plants.

Light duration

A regular period of light and dark is vital to ensure that the correct amount of photosynthesis takes place. If the lights are left on too long, plants will produce too much oxygen and literally wear themselves out. If they are left in the dark too long, they will use up energy, photosynthesis cannot take place, and oxygen levels will become diminished. Tropical regions experience roughly twelve hours of daylight (with ten hours of strong light) and ten hours of complete darkness (with two hours of dusk

Why are plants green?

Most plants appear green because the light-absorbing pigment, chlorophyll, absorbs red and blue light but does not use the green part of the spectrum – it simply reflects it, thus producing a green appearance.

Above: *Most plants require more light than is provided by a single fluorescent tube and lighting requirements will vary between species. To achieve impressive results such as this, choose both plants and lighting with care.*

and dawn). Therefore, in the aquarium, the lighting should be on for between 10 and 12 hours each day. The best way to achieve a regular lighting period is to use automatic timers to control the on/off period of individual lights. If you have a number of lights, it may be worth using a staggered approach, with each light being turned on and off in sequence, leaving a 10-15-minute gap. Because this reduces shock, it is of more benefit to the fish than the plants, which are able to adapt more quickly.

Light intensity

The intensity of a light source reaching any surface is measured in units of lux. Natural bright sunlight produces about 70,000-80,000 lux, although much of this is lost by the time it reaches aquatic plants. The lux requirement of aquarium plants varies between roughly 300 and 6,000 lux, depending on the species of plant. Plants such as *Anubias* sp. and *Cryptocoryne* sp., which are often

Many Cryptocoryne *species will do well with minimal lighting conditions in the aquarium.*

found in shaded streams, require less light than plants found on or above the water surface and in open, shallow areas, such as dwarf *Echinodorus* or *Myriophyllum*. Lux can be measured by a photographic luxmeter, although measuring lux readings in the aquarium to ensure correct light intensity is unnecessary. It is much better to start by looking at the output of light from the source.

Output of light

The output from a light source is measured in lumens. (Lux is a measure of lumens per square meter.) If the correct output of light is achieved, taking into account losses of light, it should be possible to ensure that the plants receive the correct amount of illumination. As a rough guide, a standard, rectangular planted aquarium will require about 30-50 lumens per liter of water.

Light efficiency

The efficiency of a light source can be measured by the amount of lumens produced per watt. An artificial light source uses electricity (watts) and converts it into light and heat. A fluorescent tube never gets very hot and can be touched when in use. This is because most of the electricity used is converted into light, making a fluorescent tube very efficient. On the other hand, a 60-watt household

incandescent bulb will get much hotter and will produce less light than one 60-watt (or two 30-watt) fluorescent tubes. However, this does not mean that the most efficient light source is always the best one. For larger and deeper aquariums, a number of fluorescent tubes may be needed to produce enough output (lumens). Each of these fluorescent tubes requires costly starter units and space above the aquarium. Before long, the cost and practicality of fluorescent tubes may become unwarranted and you should consider alternative light sources.

Although less efficient than fluorescent lamps, because they produce more heat and less light per watt, mercury vapor or metal halide (halogen) lamps are a good choice. Their much higher wattage ensures a higher light output and higher light intensity. Initially, these lamps may seem expensive, but compared to the equivalent light output of fluorescent tubes, they are actually a lot cheaper.

Some Echinodorus *species will grow leaves above the surface to obtain more light. This is* E. barthii.

Light spectrum

White light is made up of different colors, or wavelengths, of light. Wavelengths are measured in nanometers (nm) and the light we can see ranges between 380 and 700 nm. At one end of this "visible" spectrum is ultraviolet (UV) light, which has a wavelength of between 300 and 350 nm and at the other end is infrared light (700-750 nm). The output of different wavelengths, or colors, of light from a source is called a light spectrum, and different sources of light (sunlight, fluorescent tubes, metal halide lamps, and so on) produce different light spectrums. Light with shorter wavelengths can be considered more "energetic" than light with longer wavelengths.

Light spectrum becomes important in the aquarium when we look at how light is affected when it passes through water and how plants use it. The ability of light to penetrate water depends on how energetic it is. Energetic light with shorter wavelengths (ultraviolet light, blue light) passes through water with greater ease than less energetic light (red, infrared light), so plants are more likely to receive blue and ultraviolet light than they are red light. To maximize efficiency, plants have developed a higher photosynthetic sensitivity to red light, which may be reduced in nature, and to blue light, which is easily obtainable. Re-creating light that peaks in the red and blue areas of the spectrum can be achieved by using light sources with matching spectrums.

Do remember, however, that whereas a high blue content will promote photosynthesis, it also promotes algae growth. Algae grow predominantly in water where direct sunlight provides ample blue

"White" light

Above: By "splitting" white light through a prism, we can see it is made up of many colors, each with a different wavelength.

Ultraviolet light (300-350 nm) is of no use to plants.

Blue light has a shorter wavelength and passes through water with ease. Both plants and algae use blue light.

Aquatic plants' photosynthetic ability is most sensitive to red light between 650 and 680 nm.

Once light reaches the infrared area (700-750 nm), plants can no longer use it.

nm   400   500   600   700

light. So a suitable light source for aquarium plants should peak in the blue and, more importantly, red areas of the spectrum.

Choosing the right lighting

What we can conclude from looking at different types of light is that the best type of light depends on the function it is required to perform. Household incandescent lights are inefficient and produce a lot of heat, but are very cheap and ideal for domestic use. Fluorescent tubes are very efficient and relatively cheap if used in small numbers, ideal for smaller planted aquariums. The less efficient, but higher output/intensity lamps are ideal for larger planted aquariums. Remember that it is always better to provide too much light, rather than too little.

Many factors combine to reduce considerably the amount of light reaching plants: suspended matter, condensation trays, reflection, refraction, and simply passing through water will remove a large proportion of light. So when choosing the correct lighting for a particular system, there are four main factors to consider: efficiency (power consumption/output), output/intensity, initial cost, and light spectrum

Fluorescent, metal halide, and mercury vapor lamps are the most common sources of aquarium lighting. Here we take a closer look at each of them.

Fluorescent tubes

Fluorescent tubes emit light by electrically charging a gas contained within the tube. The light produced by the gas is mostly in the invisible areas of the spectrum, but the fluorescent coating on the inside of the tube converts this into visible light and alters its spectrum. By altering the chemical coating on the inside of the tube, the spectrum of light emitted can be changed, so fluorescent tubes can be designed for specific purposes and to emit specific colors. Fluorescent tubes designed for aquarium plant growth often produce a red-violet-blue color, which although ideal for plants, may give the tank a slightly garish look. To remedy this, full-spectrum tubes can be added to "balance" the color output.

Fluorescent tubes are the most widely used method of lighting aquariums, mainly because they are very efficient, use little electricity, and are relatively inexpensive when used in small numbers. Most fluorescent tubes will last for up to two years before they start to flicker and eventually become useless. However, their light output drops considerably within the first year of use, so the tubes become less effective and useful for plants unless they are changed at least once a year.

For smaller or shallow aquariums, fluorescent tubes are by far the best lighting solution, but for deeper or larger aquariums or for plants that require intense lighting, there are other alternatives.

Metal halide lamps

Metal halide, or halogen, lamps provide an intense, high-output light via a tungsten filament. They are ideally suited to deeper aquariums, with up to 60 cm (24 in) of water depth. The unit is suspended at least 30 cm (12 in) above the aquarium to allow ample ventilation and will illuminate approximately 1800 cm^2 (2 ft^2) of surface area. One unit will light aquariums up to 75 cm (30 in) long. Halogen lights are usually available in 150-watt and 250-watt versions; a 150-watt light should provide a suitable output for

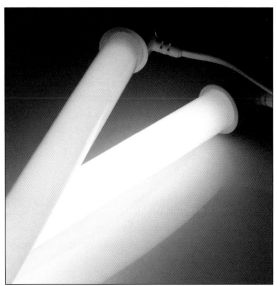

Above: Some fluorescent tubes enhance the colors of the fish, while others promote plant growth. For the best effect, use a combination of tubes.

most aquariums (250-watt versions are better suited to marine invertebrate aquariums, where demand for light from corals is higher). You may need more than one lamp for aquariums longer than 107 cm (42 in). Halogen lights are initially the most costly method of lighting, but provide the best output of light for demanding aquarium plants.

Mercury vapor lamps

Like the halogen lamps, mercury vapor lamps are suspended above the aquarium and provide a high-intensity light that is able to penetrate deeper water than fluorescent tubes. For aquariums with a depth

How many fluorescent tubes do I need?

Tank size LxDxW	No. of tubes	Tube length
60x38x30 cm (24x15x12 in)	3x15 watt	45 cm (18 in)
75x38x30 cm (30x15x12 in)	3x18-20 watt	60 cm (24 in)
90x38x30 cm (36x15x12 in)	2x25 watt	75 cm (30 in)
120x38x30 cm (48x15x12 in)	2x38 watt	107 cm (42 in)

Below: Suspending a mercury vapor or metal halide lamp above the aquarium is a good way of providing the intensity of light that some plants demand.

of 45-60 cm (18-24 in), mercury vapor lamps provide the most cost-effective and practical solution, as they are cheaper than halogen lamps and provide a much higher output than fluorescent tubes. Common mercury vapor lamps use between 60 and 125 watts, which makes them relatively low-cost to run. If they are within your budget, halogen lamps will provide the best source of light, but mercury vapor lamps are an excellent low-cost alternative.

Left: *Mercury vapor and metal halide (halogen) lamps provide the intense illumination needed to sustain red-leaved plants such as the red cabomba growing as a background plant in this aquarium.*

Other light sources

As well as fluorescent, halogen, and mercury vapor lamps, there are other, less commonly used sources. Sodium lamps and blended spotlamps are two reasonably good sources of light. Sodium lamps are efficient and long-lived, although they do lack suitable blue light and may need to be combined with an additional light source. Blended spotlamps are a combination of mercury and tungsten and provide a very well-balanced output at low cost.

Unsuitable lights include any light that does not provide suitable red or blue light and/or a low-intensity output. A typical example is the household incandescent (tungsten) bulb, which, although peaking in the red spectrum, is highly inefficient and provides little available light for aquarium plants.

Lack of adequate lighting

If the aquarium lighting is of insufficient quantity or intensity, plants will appear weak, with pale green or yellowish leaves. On some plants, leaves will grow smaller and the length of stalk between leaves (internodes) will become longer. Nearer the light, the internodes will become shorter and the leaves more compact. To remedy the situation, replace any fluorescent tubes over 12 months old, add reflectors, and make sure that the lighting is left on for at least 12-14 hours a day. Alternatively, it may be worth installing more fluorescent tubes or a new, more powerful light source. If it is only plants with red or brown leaves (except cryptocoryne) that are dying back, this may also be a sign of insufficient lighting.

Incorrect light spectrum

Many fluorescent tubes emit a high proportion of red light, which can cause plants to grow tall and thin. At the other end of the scale, too much blue light will result in shorter plants. Stunted growth and symptoms similar to those caused by a lack of adequate lighting may also be exhibited if the light spectrum is incorrect. To remedy the situation, add more lighting tubes with a spectrum that will create a better overall balance. If the plants are exhibiting symptoms of too much red light, add a tube that is high in the blue spectrum and vice versa.

Incorrect temperature

The ideal temperature for plants depends on the individual species and also on the available light, nutrients, and CO_2. Generally, at higher temperatures, plants will grow and metabolize more quickly. This means they will photosynthesize quicker, requiring adequate lighting and CO_2. Faster growth will require more nutrients. If the temperature is too high or there is not enough light, CO_2, and nutrients for the water temperature, the stem internodes become longer, the leaves smaller, and growth is inhibited. If the temperature is too low, plant growth will simply slow down, stop, and the plants will eventually die.

Aquarium plants and their lighting requirements

Very bright

Many of the plants that require high-intensity light come from shallow, open areas or have red pigments that are less efficient at photosynthesis and therefore need more light. Metal halide (halogen) lamps will provide the best source of light. For aquariums less than 45 cm (18 in) deep, mercury vapor lamps will suffice.

Alternanthera reineckii (Red hygrophila, copperleaf)
Cabomba piauhyensis (Red cabomba)
Didiplis diandra (Water hedge)
Eusteralis stellata (Star rotala)
Lilaeopsis novae zelandiae (New Zealand grassplant)
Myriophyllum mattogrossense (Red myriophyllum, red milfoil)
Rotala macrandra (Giant red rotala)
Sagittaria platyphylla (Giant sagittaria)

Bright to very bright

As above, but mercury vapor lamps will provide enough light in tanks up to 60 cm (24 in) deep.

Cardamine lyrata (Japanese cress)
Eleocharis acicularis (Hairgrass)
Nuphar japonica (Japanese spatterdock)

Bright

Most plants fit into this category and although some will grow under fluorescent tubes, for good results you would need three or four tubes or more. Ideally, use mercury vapor lamps.

Aponogeton boivinianus
Bacopa caroliniana (Giant bacopa)
Cabomba caroliniana (Green cabomba)
Ceratophyllum demersum (Hornwort)
Ceratopteris thalictroides (Indian fern)
Echinodorus cordifolius (Radicans swordplant)
Echinodorus major (Ruffled Amazon swordplant)
Echinodorus tenellus (Pygmy chain swordplant)
Gymnocoronis spilanthoides (Spadeleaf plant)
Hemigraphis colorata (Crimson ivy)
Heteranthera zosterifolia (Stargrass)
Hydrocotyle leucocephala (Water pennywort)
Hygrophila difformis (Water wisteria)
Hygrophila polysperma (Dwarf hygrophila)
Limnophila aquatica (Giant ambulia)
Ludwigia palustris (Green ludwigia)
Lysimachia nummularia 'Aurea' (Creeping Jenny, moneywort)
Myriophyllum hippuroides (Green myriophyllum, water milfoil)
Nymphaea lotus var. *rubra* (Red tiger lotus)
Pistia stratiotes (Water lettuce)
Vallisneria asiatica (Corkscrew vallisneria)
Vallisneria spiralis (Straight vallisneria)

Moderate to bright

As above. Although these plants will grow well under fluorescent light, you will need at least two or three tubes.

Anubias barteri (Broadleaf anubias)
Cryptocoryne balansae
Cryptocoryne willisii
Echinodorus bleheri (Broadleaf Amazon swordplant)
Egeria densa (Pondweed, elodea)

Moderate

These species do not require bright conditions, but will do well under stronger light if partially shaded by taller plants. Fluorescent tubes will be fine.

Aponogeton madagascariensis (Madagascan laceplant)
Bolbitis heudelotii (Congo, or African, fern)
Crinum thaianum (Onion plant)
Cryptocoryne wendtii
Riccia fluitans (Crystalwort)
Salvinia auriculata

Undemanding

Plants from naturally shaded and/or darker areas require little light. In aquariums up to 45 cm (18 in) deep, these plants could be kept with just a single fluorescent tube, although two would be better. These plants can be kept in brighter conditions, but may produce smaller, more compact leaves.

Anubias barteri var. *nana* (Dwarf anubias)
Aponogeton crispus (Wavy-edged swordplant)
Cryptocoryne beckettii
Cryptocoryne undulata (Undulate cryptocoryne)
Microsorium pteropus (Java fern)
Ophiopogon japonicum var. *giganteum*
Vesicularia dubyana (Java moss)

Feeding aquarium plants

If they are to grow properly and remain in good health, aquarium plants require carbon dioxide (CO_2) to "fuel" the process of photosynthesis (see page 8) and a number of minerals and organic nutrients, which they take in through either their leaves or roots. Supplying the correct fertilizers can be considered as giving plants a good balanced diet.

The quantity and type of fertilizers you give your plants depends on a number of factors, such as the number of fish and plants in the aquarium, the lighting, and the water temperature. Waste matter produced by fish will be used by plants as a source of food, so a well-stocked aquarium will need less additional fertilizer. On the other hand, an aquarium with good lighting and/or high temperatures will encourage plant growth, so the plants will require more nutrients.

Most fertilizers are supplied either in liquid form, for even distribution throughout the aquarium, or in tablet form, to be placed at the roots of individual plants. Before we consider those, we should look first at ways of providing a steady supply of carbon dioxide into the aquarium.

Supplying carbon dioxide

Without adequate CO_2, photosynthesis is hindered and plants are unable to perform many biological functions, such as growth, repair, and reproduction. One of the most common causes of unsuccessful plantkeeping is a lack of CO_2. No matter how good your lighting, substrate, or water quality may be, without additional CO_2 your

An aquarium carbonator

Use this bottle (fitted with the red spout) to add water to the white plastic compartment. Seal with the stopper and shake. Add the remaining water to the carbonator body and upturn the compartment in the top.

Right: Place the assembled carbonator in the aquarium. The solution in the top compartment drips through a small hole in the stopper and reacts with the white powder in the base to produce carbon dioxide gas – seen here as bubbles collecting on the inner walls.

This dome is used to collect the CO_2 gas, where it is absorbed into the water.

Pour this powder into the body of the carbonator.

Seal the compartment with this rubber stopper.

This compartment houses a reactive powder.

A weight is used to keep the unit firmly on the aquarium floor.

How a CO₂ fertilization system works

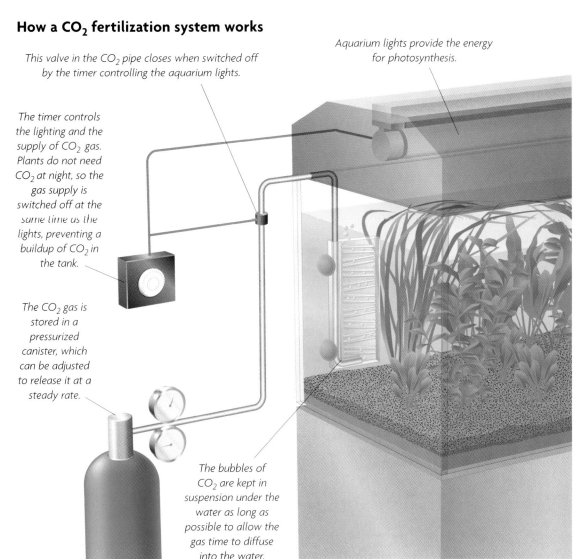

This valve in the CO_2 pipe closes when switched off by the timer controlling the aquarium lights.

Aquarium lights provide the energy for photosynthesis.

The timer controls the lighting and the supply of CO_2 gas. Plants do not need CO_2 at night, so the gas supply is switched off at the same time as the lights, preventing a buildup of CO_2 in the tank.

The CO_2 gas is stored in a pressurized canister, which can be adjusted to release it at a steady rate.

The bubbles of CO_2 are kept in suspension under the water as long as possible to allow the gas time to diffuse into the water.

plants will never reach anywhere near their full potential. And without additional CO_2, other forms of fertilization will be of little use to your plants.

You can introduce CO_2 into the aquarium in a number of ways. One is a simple chemical-based system, whereby a reaction between two compounds in a plastic container gradually releases CO_2 (see page 32) and this is absorbed by the water. This type of system is fine for increasing the amount of CO_2 available to plants, but it offers no way of controlling the amount of CO_2 introduced.

For a larger aquarium, where the plants are the main concern, there are a number of elaborate and impressive systems tailored to providing exactly the right amounts of CO_2 at the times when the plants need them most. The majority of these systems (see opposite) involve a gradual and controlled release of CO_2 from a compressed cylinder situated outside the aquarium. Because plants only photosynthesize during daylight hours, they need no additional CO_2 at night, and it is possible to obtain CO_2 cylinder systems that can be controlled by the aquarium lighting, releasing CO_2 only when the lights are on.

Liquid fertilizers

Possibly the most common method of fertilization is by means of a liquid fertilizer. This is easy to use and gives the entire plant community all the necessary nutrients in a readily available form. It is also the easiest way to overfertilize the aquarium, so be sure to follow the manufacturer's recommendations (although these can be adjusted to suit your aquarium's needs). Most liquid nutrients are present in a form available to the plants for only a few weeks, so regular dosing is needed. The best time to add liquid fertilizer is just after a water change, thus ensuring that nutrient levels are kept at an optimum.

Tablet fertilizers

Although liquid and substrate fertilization will give the entire plant community a balanced source of nutrients, there may be instances when individual plants need an extra "boost." This is when tablet fertilizers are useful. They can be placed directly beside or underneath the roots of individual plants, allowing single plants to access the nutrients. You can break up the tablets and distribute the pieces to feed plants over a wider area. Tablet fertilizers may continue to release nutrients for periods ranging from a few weeks to several months, depending on the type you choose. The ability to fertilize individual plants can be useful when you add new plants to the aquarium, as it helps them to settle in quickly. Other plants simply require more nutrients.

Slow-release substrate fertilizers

Using a nutrient-rich substrate, such as a clay-based material or specially designed planting substrate, is a form of slow-release fertilization. This kind of substrate is usually added as a thin layer sandwiched between two layers of inert substrate (see page 21). The plants then have a constant supply of key nutrients such as iron, which they can absorb as and when necessary through their root systems. Slow-release substrate fertilization is an ideal "safe" method of fertilization.

Below: This recently positioned plant will soon be able to absorb nutrients directly from the area around the fertilizer tablet, giving it a much-needed boost. Place fertilizer tablets directly under or close to the roots of individual plants.

This liquid fertilizer is supplied with a measuring lid for accurate dosing. Follow the directions provided with each manufacturer's product.

Left: Liquid fertilizers added regularly to the aquarium will provide plants with a wide range of nutrients. Be careful not to overdose, which may cause algal blooms.

Tablet fertilizers last longer but release nutrients only into the area immediately surrounding the plant.

Due to the slow-release process, healthy plants will use up the nutrients as they become available, thus eliminating the chances of "overdosing" the aquarium with nutrients. Most nutrient-rich substrates will lose part or most of their nutrients within three years, at which point they will need replacing.

Using fertilizers correctly

Adding fertilizers to the aquarium will certainly be of great benefit to your plants, but only if it is done correctly and in the right quantities. It is important to achieve a good balance and a regular feeding regime: Too little fertilizer and plant growth will slow down and leaves will become unhealthy, too much and algae will bloom on the excess nutrients. Unfortunately, it is not easy to keep track of the levels of various nutrients in the aquarium. Test kits are available for common nutrients, such as iron, potassium, phosphate, and carbon dioxide, and these may be worth investing in for larger aquariums.

Nutrient-rich substrates contain a number of materials that slowly release specific nutrients and minerals.

Nutritional problems

Fertilizers provide plants with substances that are not always available in sufficient quantities from the aquarium water. If a plant becomes unhealthy due to a lack, or excess, of one or more of these substances, the result can be described as a nutritional problem.

CO_2 deficiency Supplying adequate (or additional) carbon dioxide is vital for good plant health, and one of the main reasons why plants do not do well in the aquarium is because they lack CO_2. Without adequate CO_2, plants will grow more slowly, are smaller, and, in extreme cases, will exhibit a white, chalky deposit on the leaves. If little CO_2 is being introduced to the aquarium, it is important to minimize the surface agitation, because this is where CO_2 is lost from the water. Remove any airstones and make sure the filter outlet is about 10 cm (4 in) below the water surface. Fertilize with CO_2.

Potassium deficiency Potassium is present in many liquid fertilizers, so as long as the aquarium is regularly fertilized, there should be no problem. However, if potassium is not added (in the form of plant fertilizers) it is rarely available to plants, because most tapwater contains little or no potassium. Because of this, potassium deficiency is quite common in many aquariums and can be seen as a yellowing around the edges of new leaves and weaker-looking leaves.

Iron deficiency Of all the nutrients essential for good plant health, iron is the most important and is used in the most abundance by plants. A lack of iron will result in distinctly yellowish, thin leaves with light-colored veins that will in time begin to break down and die. A good, nutrient-rich layer of substrate combined with regular fertilization with an iron-rich fertilizer should prevent this problem from occurring.

The pale leaves on this Hygrophila *sp. are typical signs of iron deficiency which, if not remedied, may kill the plant.*

Manganese deficiency Manganese is another important nutrient. The symptoms of manganese deficiency are similar to those of iron deficiency. Leaves become yellowish, but the leaf veins remain green or dark green.

Chelated nutrients

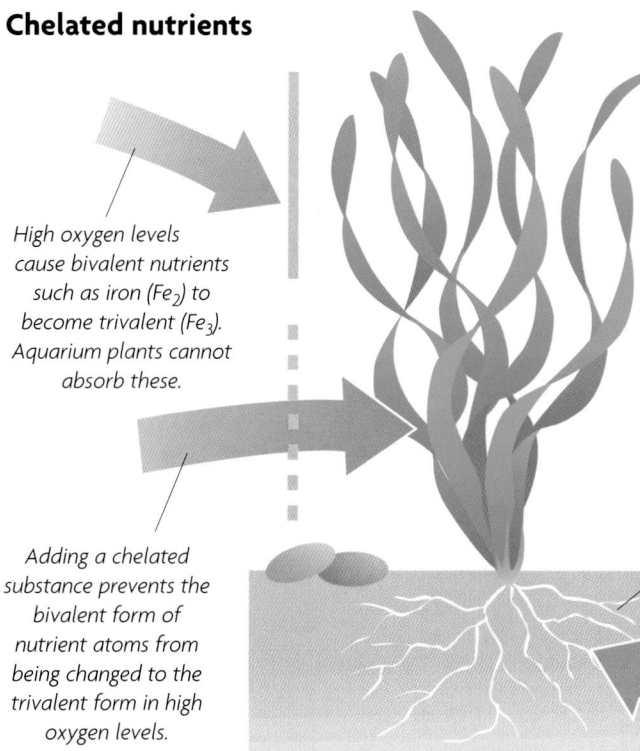

High oxygen levels cause bivalent nutrients such as iron (Fe_2) to become trivalent (Fe_3). Aquarium plants cannot absorb these.

Adding a chelated substance prevents the bivalent form of nutrient atoms from being changed to the trivalent form in high oxygen levels.

Chelated nutrients

As we have seen in the section on plant biology (pages 8-11), aquatic plants do not appreciate high oxygen levels. One of the main reasons for this is that oxygen can reduce a plant's ability to make use of nutrients available in the water and in the substrate. Plants absorb nutrients through either the leaves or the roots and this happens via cells that allow molecules up to a certain size to pass through the cell wall. There is a limit to the size of molecule that can be absorbed through the cell wall to prevent useful substances from passing out and to keep the structure of each cell intact.

Nutrients in the aquarium can be found in two forms, bivalent and trivalent. The bivalent form is water-soluble and small enough to be absorbed readily by plants.

Most nutrients are absorbed through the plant roots, although some are taken in by the leaves.

The low oxygen conditions in the substrate mean that the nutrients remain in the usable bivalent form.

Fertilizing aquarium plants accurately

Following a few simple tips should help to ensure that you fertilize your aquarium plants accurately and achieve the best results.

A turbulent water surface will reduce the amount of CO_2 the aquarium can hold. Try to ensure that the filter outflow is situated at least 10 cm (4 in) below the water surface. Avoid any unnecessary aeration.

If you are using tapwater and a nutrient-rich (slow-release) substrate, you may not need to use a liquid fertilizer. Tapwater often contains many of the key nutrients that plants require. Rainwater and R.O. (Reverse Osmosis) water are virtually devoid of nutrients and liquid fertilizer is a must.

Add only fertilizers specifically designed for aquarium use. Terrestrial plant fertilizers contain excess nitrates and chemicals that may be harmful to fish and/or aquatic plants.

Never use adsorptive filter media, such as activated carbon, unless for a specific (short-term) reason, as these will remove useful nutrients.

Regardless of nitrate levels, carry out regular small water changes to remove and replenish nutrients.

It is always better to introduce regular, small doses of fertilizers than irregular or infrequent large doses.

The trivalent form is larger and plants cannot absorb it, making the nutrient useless. In water with oxygen levels above 2 mg/liter, a bivalent nutrient such as iron (bivalent form, Fe_2) has a tendency to bond with other iron atoms, using oxygen, and creating a trivalent form (Fe_3). The obvious solution to this problem would be to reduce oxygen levels to below 2 mg/liter, but few fish could live in such a low-oxygen environment and biological filtration would be impaired. Most liquid fertilizers now available contain organic substances called chelates, which help to prevent this problem. Chelates will attach themselves to bivalent nutrients such as iron (Fe_2) and prevent oxygen from bonding nutrients together, thus preventing trivalent nutrients from forming. The bivalent nutrient is now larger, but still small enough to be readily absorbed by plants. Although chelates are added to most liquid fertilizers, in high-oxygen conditions they become less effective so it is still important to prevent high oxygen conditions in the planted aquarium.

This leaf is fairly young, yet obviously in bad condition. Algae on the leaf show a lack of growth.

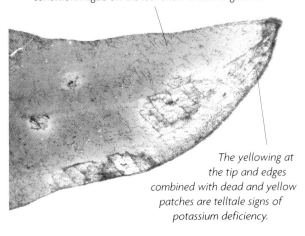

The yellowing at the tip and edges combined with dead and yellow patches are telltale signs of potassium deficiency.

Signs of nutritional problems

To help you identify problems, there are a number of signs to look for, either on the plants or in the aquarium. More often than not, it is a combination of problems that produces a certain effect on aquarium plants. Algal blooms, for instance, may indicate an overdosing of nutrients in general rather than of one specific nutrient.

Nutrient	Symptom of deficiency	Symptom of excess
Calcium	New leaves misshapen or stunted. Existing leaves remain green.	Rise in pH and/or hardness level.
Carbon dioxide	White chalky deposit on leaves. Stunted growth. Individual plants die back.	Fish gasping at the water surface.
Iron	Young leaves are yellow/white, with green veins. Mature leaves are normal.	Excess iron can cause manganese deficiency.
Magnesium	Lower leaves turn yellow from tip inward. Veins remain green.	–
Manganese	Yellow spots between veins. Elongated holes between veins. Manganese deficiency can be caused by excess iron.	–
Nitrates	Growth may become slow or stunted.	Algal bloom in tank.
Nitrogen	Upper leaves light green. Lower leaves yellow. Bottom (older) leaves yellow and shriveled.	Small brown spots on older leaves
Phosphate	Leaves darker than normal. Loss of leaves.	Algal bloom in tank.
Potassium	Yellowing at tips and edges, especially on young leaves. Dead or yellow patches or spots develop on leaves.	–

Aquarium plants can be propagated in two ways: sexual and asexual. Sexual propagation involves taking two parent plants and combining the genetic information using their flowers and seeds or spores to produce a number of new and genetically different plants. This method requires plants to produce flowers above the water surface, and many species will readily achieve this in the aquarium. However, to produce viable seed the flowers must be pollinated, but unfortunately, this is unlikely to occur in the home aquarium without outside help. Producing new plants through sexual propagation is time-consuming and difficult, so in this book we will concentrate on methods of propagation involving asexual reproduction.

Asexual propagation requires only a single plant and involves the production of new, or "daughter," plants. This can be achieved by a number of methods depending on the species of plant. Many species will quickly propagate themselves given the correct conditions; others will require the direct intervention of the aquarist.

Runners

Many common aquarium plants produce new plantlets by means of runners. A horizontal, stemlike shoot (a runner) is produced at the base of the plant and grows just above or below the substrate surface. A small daughter plant, or "slip," is produced at the end of the runner and soon forms new leaves and roots. Many plants will produce a series of slips along one runner. The individual slips will produce roots while still obtaining nutrients from the main

Propagating from a runner

1 Once the "mother" plant has produced a number of daughter plants with at least two or three leaves, the runner can be cut with a pair of sharp scissors. This is Echinodorus sp.

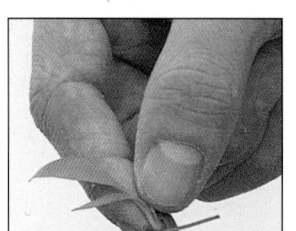

2 Separate the individual plants, or "slips," leaving a small length of runner on either side. The plants are very small, so handle them extremely carefully, holding them by the leaf and not by the stem.

3 Put each new plant into the substrate, as described on page 24, leaving a gap of at least 5 cm (2 in) between the plants to allow for future growth.

Propagating from cuttings

1 To take a top cutting, snip off a length of stem with several leaves or nodes. Cut between nodes with a pair of sharp scissors.

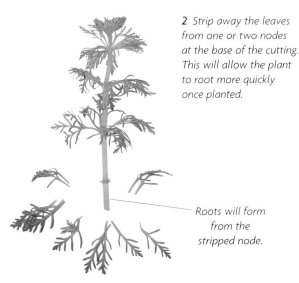

2 Strip away the leaves from one or two nodes at the base of the cutting. This will allow the plant to root more quickly once planted.

Roots will form from the stripped node.

plant through the runner. If left to develop, the runners between each slip eventually break down and the plants will become unconnected.

To slow down the rate of propagation or to relocate the new plants, you can cut the runners and separate the plants. A new plant can be separated from its "parent" as soon as it has produced leaves or shoots, although early separation will reduce the number of slips produced from the original plant. It is best to wait until the new plants have produced

3 Push the cutting into the substrate so that the lower leaves are just resting on the substrate surface. Roots should grow from the base and the plant will establish quickly.

two or three leaves and are at least 3-4 cm (1.2-1.6 in) high. In the case of some *Cryptocoryne* sp., it is best to wait until the plant is about a quarter to half the size of the adult plant. If you wish to produce more plants, simply leave the runners alone to continue producing new slips, which can be planted while still attached to the runners.

Common species that propagate by runners include *Vallisneria, Echinodorus, Cryptocoryne, Sagittaria*, and some species of floating plant.

Cuttings

Any plant with a central stem from which leaves are produced can be propagated by taking cuttings. Many aquatic plants are sold in the form of cuttings taken from well-established plants, and the process is similar to taking cuttings from terrestrial plants.

Cuttings can be taken from sideshoots or from the top and middle sections of a plant, although the top section, being the part of the plant that is already growing, will establish more quickly once planted.

The points at which leaves are produced from a stem are called "nodes" and at least three or four nodes should be present on each cutting. Using a pair of sharp scissors, cut a section of the stem and remove any leaves from the bottom one or two nodes. This is where the roots will form. Plant the cutting in the substrate, covering these bottom nodes. It should produce roots and continue to grow within a week or two. The original plant will produce new sideshoots from the uppermost node or nodes and continue to grow. Because it usually produces two or more sideshoots, taking cuttings can be used as a method of producing thicker, bushier growth.

Species of *Hygrophila, Alternanthera, Cabomba, Egeria*, and *Ludwigia* can all be propagated by taking cuttings in this way.

Rhizomes

A rhizome is a modified stem that appears as a thick root at the base of the plant. Rhizomes are often used by plants as a means of storage, as well as for the production of new shoots. To produce new

Below: The rhizome of this African fern (Bolbitis heudelotii) *is clearly visible. A new shoot to the right of the rhizome indicates that this is the growing end and the best area from which to take a cutting.*

plants, cut the rhizome with a sharp knife and divide it, ensuring that each division contains at least one good shoot. Then replant the divisions in the tank.

Before you can cut the rhizome, you will need to remove the original plant from the substrate. Do this carefully, so that the roots are not damaged. If the original plant or any cuttings or divisions have a large amount of rootstock, trim this back so that it is about 2.5 cm (1 in) long before replanting. Trimming the roots will reduce the amount of damage caused by replanting and ensures that the plant will quickly develop fresh, new roots.

Species of *Bolbitis, Nuphar, Microsorium*, and *Anubias* can be propagated from rhizomes.

Plants such as Java fern *(Microsorium pteropus)* and some *Anubias* sp. prefer to be planted on rocks and wood. In these cases, you can take cuttings directly from the rootstock without removing the plant from the rock or wood. Only the trailing roots of the new cutting need to be trimmed. As it was not planted in the substrate, the original rootstock should not be damaged.

Adventitious plantlets

Many aquarium plants develop small, fully formed plantlets on stem nodes, leaves, and roots. If left alone, these plantlets eventually detach and root themselves in the substrate. Alternatively, once a plantlet has developed five or six leaves and a few small roots, you can remove it from its "parent" and plant it in the substrate. Some fernlike plants, such as Java fern, produce numerous adventitious plantlets. These are best left to detach naturally, at which

point you can collect and plant them as required. Species of *Echinodorus, Microsorium, Ceratopteris, Aponogeton*, and many other plants can be easily propagated from adventitious plantlets.

Above: New plantlets with well-developed roots are clearly visible at the tip of this Java fern leaf. You can either separate and replant these or leave them to develop and drop off naturally.

Offsets

Plants that grow in clumps, with leaves forming from the base, often produce new plants at the root. These offsets are formed in a similar way to plantlets from runners, except that they grow much closer to the original plant. A large plant may actually contain a number of offsets, which can be gently divided and replanted elsewhere.

Species of *Acorus, Cryptocoryne*, and *Echinodorus* can be successfully propagated from offsets.

Propagating from adventitious plantlets

1 The plantlets underneath this leaf are well developed, while the "mother" leaf is beginning to die to allow the plantlets to drop off. This makes them easier to remove by hand and plant separately. This plant is a Java fern.

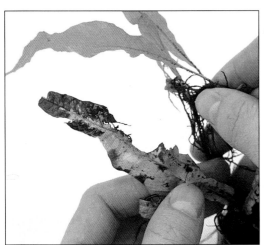

2 The new plantlet is now large enough to be replanted. Simply pull it from the main leaf. As the "mother" leaf is beginning to fall apart, remove it from the main plant and discard it.

3 This plantlet is "fully fledged," with a number of large leaves and trailing roots. Trim the roots to a length of about 2.5 cm (1 in) before replanting.

4 One leaf may produce several plantlets in close proximity. When removing plantlets, check carefully to see how many individual plants there are. Even quite small plantlets can be separated and replanted.

41

Keeping aquarium plants healthy

If left unattended, a planted aquarium can quickly become a tangled mess of vegetation. Fast-growing plants will collect together at the surface, blocking out the light to smaller, slower species, and waste matter will build up, causing a decline in water quality. However, maintenance need not be time-consuming; if it is planned and carried out regularly, it may take as little as 30 minutes a week and the results will be rewarding and well worth the effort. As well as attending to the aquarium plants, it is important to acknowledge that all the other aspects of the aquarium – lighting, filtration, water quality, the substrate, and fish health – are just as important. Every aquarium will have individual needs, so it is best to follow a standard guideline and adapt it to suit the requirements of your system. Some items will need less maintenance, others more.

Moving and replanting aquarium plants

Over time, plants will spread and move around. Some will grow until they dwarf others or you may wish to vary the display slightly; in each case you will need to move and replant some species. Moving a plant can be quite damaging to the rootstock and can affect the overall health of a plant, especially if it is well established. It is important to minimize this damage. When

Right: Keeping a display healthy requires regular pruning, replanting, and general care and attention. Spend time at least once a week on your plants, removing dead leaves and debris to ensure that the display remains at its best.

Routine maintenance in the aquarium

Daily
- Check for any missing livestock and examine the health of all the fish. Look for red marks on the body and gills, excess mucus, gasping, or unusual behavior.
- Check the water temperature.
- Make sure that the filter(s) and lights are working.

Twice weekly
- Gently disturb any fine-leaved plants, such as cabomba, and dense foreground species, such as hairgrass, to remove any trapped detritus, which can hinder photosynthesis.

Weekly
- Test the water for nitrites (NO_2), nitrates (NO_3), pH, and hardness.
- Remove dead leaves and other plant matter.
- Siphon out or remove any mulm from the top layer of substrate and replace the water removed during this process with new, dechlorinated water. This will also constitute a small water change, replacing minerals and helping to lower nitrates and phosphates.
- Replenish liquid fertilizers after water changes according to the manufacturer's instructions.
- Using an algae magnet, pad, or scraper, clean the inside front and side glass, even if little algae is present. This prevents a buildup of algae that is hard to remove.
- If you have a condensation cover, wipe it clean to avoid a reduction in light penetration.

Every two weeks
- Thoroughly clean half the sponge in the internal filter, using water from the aquarium. Then drain it away.

Monthly
- Switch off external filters and clean the media in water from the aquarium. Then drain the water away.
- Replace any filter floss in an external filter.

Every three months
- Check the substrate for compaction and gently loosen it with your fingers.
- Remove and clean any impellers and impeller housings in pumps and filters.

Every 6-12 months
- If fluorescent tubes are the main source of lighting, replace them even if they are still working; after 10-12 months they will have lost much of their intensity.
- Replace filter sponges. Over time, the bacterial capacity of sponges will diminish and they will need to be replaced. If sponges are the main biological medium, then replace half at a time, leaving a month in between. This will reduce the loss of bacteria.

When needed
- Replenish liquid or tablet fertilizers according to the manufacturer's instructions.
- Check and replenish any CO_2 supply systems that may be in use in the aquarium.
- Trim any tall stem plants so that they do not grow across the surface and block out light to other plants. Replant the cuttings if you wish.
- If tall-stemmed plants are looking thin near the base, remove them, cut off the upper halves, and replant.
- If the leaves of plants such as large Echinodorus sp. have grown too big, remove the outermost leaves and trim the roots slightly. The plant will respond by producing fresh, smaller leaves.
- Old plant leaves may become tattered or covered in algae. Remove them to prevent the spread of algae and to allow new leaves to grow.
- Over time, some plants will become old and begin to look less healthy. They stop growing and become tattered. If this happens, remove and replace them. Be sure to take out the entire rootstock, as any pieces left over may rot and pollute the substrate.

Below: Trimming tall stem plants regularly will help to keep a tidy aquarium and create a shorter, bushier plant. Top cuttings can also be replanted in the aquarium (see page 39).

removing a plant, take out as much of the rootstock as possible. Work carefully; using your fingers, you should be able to feel where the roots are and how large the root system is. Gently "tease out" the roots without disturbing too much of the substrate (which may be made up of different layers).

Once you have the whole plant in your hand, trim the roots until they are just a few centimeters long. This ensures that when they are replanted, you minimize the damage caused by pushing them into the substrate. The plant will be able to grow new, fresh roots and can recover quickly.

Replant as normal, creating a dip in the substrate, and pack the substrate around the roots. Place an iron-rich fertilizer tablet just below the plant or close by the roots to get the plant off to a good start in its new position.

Plant diseases

It is rare for plants to suffer from disease and apart from cryptocoryne rot there are no common plant diseases that regularly affect aquarium plants. If there are visible signs of plant ill-health, they are most likely to be related to an environmental or nutritional factor. Providing the problem can be identified and remedied in time, plants usually recover very quickly.

These holes may appear to be snail damage, but the condition of the whole leaf indicates a more serious problem.

Cryptocoryne rot is a condition that, as its name suggests, affects *Cryptocoryne* species. It is common in many aquariums, although its cause is not entirely clear. Initially, you may notice small holes in the leaves or leaf edges, as if snails or fish have been eating them. If the problem persists, the whole plant eventually breaks down and dies. The major cause is a change of environment once a plant has become established, but high nitrate levels, inadequate lighting, lack of water changes, and incorrect nutrients may also be contributing factors. The condition is not too serious and plants usually recover quickly once water quality is improved and/or the plant becomes re-established. Once again, the key to prevention is good and regular maintenance of the aquarium environment.

This plant may be experiencing cryptocoryne rot. Providing conditions within the aquarium are good, new leaves should not have the same problem.

Poisoning

Some aquarium treatments are harmful to aquatic plant life and can cause serious damage, even in small amounts. Such damage may take the form of a random degeneration of plant tissue, such as thinning leaves, holes, and generally ill-looking plants. Most chemical treatments designed for aquarium use are relatively safe; if they are potentially harmful, this should be clearly stated on the product. Use chemicals only when necessary and not as a preventative. It is a good idea to use chemical filtration media, such as activated carbon, to remove chemicals from the water when they are no longer needed. Of particular harm to plants are chemicals found in some algicides, and the foul-smelling gas hydrogen sulphide, which is often produced in compacted, anaerobic substrates. Over-fertilization of plants can also cause poisoning by certain otherwise useful substances.

These yellow areas may be signs of poisoning or a lack of iron. Poisoned plants degenerate more quickly than those short of nutrients.

Snails in the aquarium

Whether or not snails are damaging in the aquarium depends on the number present. Snails can enter the aquarium environment via a number of routes and will breed quickly, often becoming an unsightly addition to the display. The most common route for snails to enter the aquarium is via live plants. Most live plants now available are relatively snail-free, but it is always best to check them thoroughly first. It is possible to "dip" aquarium plants in a brand name chemical before introducing them into the aquarium to kill any snails. Avoid plants from ponds or any other outside source; you risk introducing not only snails, but also other pests and aquatic diseases.

If snails are an existing problem, remove them by hand and control their breeding by reducing the amount of organic waste in the tank by regular gravel cleaning. You can also keep snail-eating fish, such as clown loaches. Use brand name snail killers with extreme caution, as they may be based on metals that are dangerous to some delicate fish and will adversely affect and even kill some plants.

Are fish eating my plants?

One of the most common problems experienced by new fishkeepers is fish eating aquarium plants. Although some fish are heavily herbivorous (see page 48), the majority will not cause any major harm to plants if the conditions for plant growth are good and the plants are healthy. It is much more likely that the problem lies elsewhere and it simply appears that the fish are eating the plants.

Above: The tinfoil barb (Barbodes schwanenfeldii) can grow quite large and, being an active fish, could cause a great deal of damage in a planted aquarium.

Leaf damage from the center outward and little yellowing of leaves is an indication of snail damage.

Below: Once a couple of snails start to lay eggs, a population boom may be the result. Hundreds of snails together could cause a good deal of harm to aquatic plants. The eggs appear as blobs of jelly on the leaves.

Keeping aquarium plants healthy

Algae in the aquarium

Algae will grow in one form or another in all aquariums. Wherever there is water, light, and a source of nutrients, there will be algae. Small amounts of slow-growing algae on wood, rocks, and larger plant leaves will cause no problems; in fact, they will provide food for some fish, while adding a natural appearance to the aquarium decor.

Problems with algae occur when conditions in the aquarium environment become ideal for rapid algae growth. The conditions are discussed below. In this event, an algal bloom may occur that can quickly swamp plants and decor — in the worst cases, literally choking the aquarium by preventing light from reaching plants and releasing dangerous gases into the water. It is impossible to prevent algae from entering the aquarium, but it is possible to prevent algal blooms and control algae growth through good aquarium management.

Single-celled algae If the water turns a green color, it is likely to be as a result of single-celled algae. Green water will not be removed by increased filtration, as is often thought, since the individual algal cells are far too small to be trapped by the filter media used in most filtration systems.

Single-celled algae are the result of too much light (almost always sunlight) reaching the tank and the presence of excess organic matter, such as uneaten food in the aquarium.
Treatment: Reduce the amount of light reaching the aquarium and keep a careful check on feeding. Changing the water will not help, as the fresh, new

water will simply encourage the algae to bloom again by replacing used nutrients. Chemical treatments are available that work by "clumping" the algae, so that they form larger particles that will then either sink or become trapped in the filter media.

Filamentous algae Also known as blanketweed, thread algae, and hair algae, this fibrous green algae will cover plants and decor, resulting in an unsightly problem that is hard to eliminate. Sunlight or incorrect lighting, combined with an excess of organic material in the aquarium may cause this type of algae to bloom.
Treatment: The best solution is to physically remove as much algae as possible and follow this with a thorough gravel clean (see maintenance, page 43). Chemical treatments may not be effective.

Below: Filamentous algae can quickly cover any surface, causing massive damage to plants and ruining a display. Try to stop this algae before it becomes uncontrollable.

Preventing algae in the aquarium

There are a few steps you can take to avoid a proliferation of unwanted algae. Provided these are followed and fertilization is not excessive, algae should be easy to control. It is quite common to experience small algal blooms in a new aquarium, although these should go away within a few weeks.

Introduce a group of small algae-eaters, such as Otocinclus sp. and/or loaches and suckermouth catfish. Stick to smaller species to avoid disruption.

Avoid direct sunlight at all costs; even the best-kept aquarium will succumb to algal blooms if placed in direct sunlight.

Make sure the aquarium receives no more than 12 hours of artificial lighting per day. If possible, introduce a midday "siesta" period (see page 27).

Be sure to use the correct spectrum and intensity of lighting units in the aquarium.

Clean the gravel regularly using a gravel siphon to reduce the buildup of organic material.

Carry out regular small water changes to reduce the buildup of nitrates and phosphates in the aquarium.

Avoid overdosing the water with liquid nutrients and do not use fertilizers containing phosphates.

Blue-green algae This algae will form a thin blanket across any surface, and feels slimy. A form of it can occasionally be seen as surface scum. The algae also has a distinctive smell that often emanates from the water. It is often caused by high nutrient levels and bad water quality.
Treatment: Blue-green algae can be removed easily with a siphon, but will quickly regrow. Use chemical media, such as activated carbon, and add less liquid fertilizer to reduce nutrient levels. Virtually no algae-eating fish will eat blue-green algae.

Brown algae Although often called brown algae, this is not one of the true brown algae that are found in salt water. This algae will grow on the aquarium glass and, providing it is cleaned regularly, will not cause a problem. It cannot be attributed to any specific cause, but occurs more in aquariums with hard water or low light levels.
Treatment: The algae is easy to remove; simply wipe it with a suitable aquarium cleaning pad. The best method of control is to use algae-eating fish.

Brush algae This is usually found on plant leaves or on bogwood. It consists of small, furlike tufts, no more than 1cm (0.4 in) high and black or brown in color. There are no special conditions that encourage this algae to grow, but once established it will slowly spread and become unsightly.
Treatment: The only reliable remedy is to completely remove any objects on which the algae has settled. Very few brand name chemical treatments will claim to remove brush algae.

Above: *Small algae-eating fish, such as this dwarf otocinclus (Otocinclus affinis), will constantly clean algae off rocks, substrate, and leaves, so include them in every planted aquarium.*

Left: *Once leaves become old and slow growing, algae will begin to form on them. Depending on the severity of algae growth and the condition of the leaves, remove them, allowing new ones to grow.*

Right: *By cleaning the glass regularly, even when it appears relatively clean, you can avoid a buildup of algae. If you have algae-eating fish, clean only the front glass, leaving a source of food on the other panes.*

The ideal conditions required by plants in the aquarium are not always the same as those for the fish, which begs the question: How do they live together happily in nature? The simple answer is that an "ideal" planted aquarium environment is not the same as the environment in which plants are found in nature. In the aquarium, there are often many species of plant with varying needs; conditions have to be "optimized" to cater to all of them. However, in nature, there may only be two or three dominant species of plant within a long stretch of river, because the prevailing conditions may be suited to only those few species.

In the massive amounts of water found in natural locations, there are only minimal amounts of nutrients and CO_2, but these are constantly replenished and always available to the plants. If the same low levels of nutrients and CO_2 existed in the aquarium, they would quickly become exhausted and the plants would begin to suffer and die back. So "ideal" plant conditions in the aquarium would have to include a plentiful supply of CO_2 and nutrients, far above natural levels, and low oxygen levels to prevent the loss of these two factors. However, low oxygen levels and excess CO_2 do not represent ideal conditions for many fish.

Not only does the "ideal" plant environment present problems for some fish, but certain fish can cause problems for plants. For many fish, vegetation is an important part of their diet and a few are almost completely herbivorous. A group of herbivorous fish in a planted aquarium could cause a great deal of damage relatively quickly if given a chance. Certain fish, particularly some of the medium to large Central American cichlids, are naturally boisterous. They may simply be marking territories or establishing nesting or breeding sites, but they can be destructive. And large, active fish,

Common herbivorous fish to avoid

Abramites *sp. (headstanders)*
Distichodus *sp.*
Leporinus *sp.*
Metynnis *sp. (silver dollars)*
Scatophagus *sp. (scats)*

Common large, boisterous, or destructive fish to avoid:

Barbodes schwanenfeldii *(tinfoil barb)*
Larger barbs
Central American cichlids
Rift Lake cichlids
Pterygoplichthys / Glyptoperichthys *sp.*
Serrasalmus *sp. (piranhas)*
Large Synodontis *sp.*

Left: *Many livebearers, including these mollies (Poecilia sp.), prefer harder water, whereas most plants do better in soft water. By carefully selecting plants that will live in slightly harder water, you can ensure that the two can be kept together happily.*

such as the bigger barbs or cichlids, can easily damage delicate plants simply by being clumsy.

Providing you select the fish for a planted aquarium with care, the two will live together happily in the aquarium under the same conditions. In fact, the right fish and plants will complement each other; the plants will help to remove toxins from the water and act as a form of natural filtration, while the fish will help to remove dead or dying leaves and algae from the plants and produce waste that will act as a fertilizer for them.

Suitable fish for planted aquariums

Suitable fish are generally species that are neither too large nor too active. Active fish require higher oxygen levels than slower-moving fish, so may not be suited to the low-oxygen environment. Larger fish, such as some gouramis, can be included as they are generally slow moving and possess an organ that allows them to "breathe" atmospheric air.

Small barbs, such as Puntius tetrazona *(tiger barb),* Puntius titteya *(cherry barb), and* Puntius oligolepis *(checker barb)*

Dwarf cichlids, such as Apistogramma *sp. and* Pelvicachromis pulcher *(kribensis)*

Farlowella *sp.*

Killifish

Labyrinth fish, such as gouramis

Rainbowfish

Any small rasbora species, such as Trigostoma heteromorpha *(harlequin rasbora)*

Small tetras, such as Hemigrammus bleheri *(rummy-nose tetra) and* Paracheirodon axelrodi *(cardinal tetra)*

Left: *The cardinal tetra (Paracheirodon axelrodi) is a small schooling fish that does best in a well-planted aquarium, where it can find plenty of shelter.*

Below: *Small, scavenging catfish such as these Corydoras sp. will constantly disturb the top layer of substrate, usefully removing waste food and loosening debris.*

Below: *Gouramis, such as this dwarf gourami (Colisa lalia), are quite happy in low-oxygen conditions, as their labyrinth organ enables them to take in atmospheric air at the water surface and extract the oxygen.*

Useful fish for planted aquariums

Useful fish include species that eat algae as their main or only diet without harming plants and other fish, and those that will gently disturb the substrate, such as small, bottom-dwelling scavengers, because they help to prevent compaction and stagnation.

Corydoras *sp.*

Crossocheilus siamensis *(Siamese flying fox)*

Gyrinocheilus aymonieri *(sucking loach, or Indian algae-eater)*

Otocinclus affinis *(dwarf otocinclus)*

Pangio kuhlii *(coolie loach)*

Peckoltia *sp. (dwarf peckoltias)*

Poecilia *sp. (mollies)*

Plants for the aquarium

Finding a suitable site for the aquarium is essential, as a tank full of water will be very hard to move. Choose a spot away from direct sunlight and away from noise and vibration. Provide a suitably strong base and check that the floor is strong enough to take the weight. Place a foam pad or a layer of polystyrene between the tank and stand or cabinet to avoid cracking the base. You will need a power source nearby and room around the back of and above the tank for cables, pipes, and maintenance. Avoid locating the tank near heat sources such as radiators, and steer clear of busy areas, such as hallways or doorways, to minimize disruption.

Planning the display

Planning should involve selecting suitable fish, plants, and decor, and sketching out a rough design. Try to imagine how the plants will look in the aquarium and allocate spaces for groups of plants in an overhead view. Bear in mind any equipment or budget restrictions. For example, if the lighting is restricted to fluorescent tubes, then plants requiring little light, such as cryptocorynes, would be ideal, whereas cabomba or red plants would not thrive. Adopt a steady approach to choosing and buying your plants, working out which plants and how many of them will look best in your aquarium. Also consider whether they suit the water conditions in your area.

Select a mixture of background, midground, and foreground plants, along with a few specimen and floating plants if you wish. Most plants look best when grouped together, so there is no need to have a wide variety of species in the aquarium.

Left: Separating background and foreground plants using rocks or bogwood is a good way of creating a sense of depth in the aquarium display. There are different types of bogwood to choose from, but it is usually better to stick to one type. Bogwood shaped like twisted roots looks highly effective positioned vertically and poking out of the vegetation.

Degrees of difficulty

1-2: Suitable for beginners
Plants with no specific requirements that will do well with a reasonably good substrate, CO_2, and fluorescent lighting.

2-3: May have special requirements
Easy to keep, but may have individual needs, such as bright lighting, additional iron, or specific substrates.

3-4: Experience required
More delicate species that may have specific needs in addition to good water quality, lighting, substrate, and fertilizers.

Sketching a plan

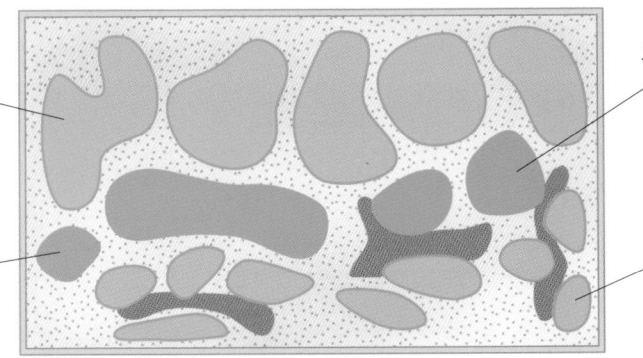

BACKGROUND
Place tall and/or bushy plants in large groups toward the back.

BACK- /MIDGROUND
Stem plants or plants on bogwood make good middle to background plants.

SPECIMEN/UNUSUAL
Single large-species plants may require their own space as display plants.

FOREGROUND
Smaller plants can be placed among small rocks/pebbles and bogwood at the front of the aquarium.

Key to plant types

BG: *Background*
B/MG: *Back- /Midground*
FG: *Foreground*
FL: *Floating*
SU: *Specimen/Unusual*
NA: *Nonaquatic*

*Below: Stargrass
(Heteranthera
zosterifolia) is a
bushy plant. Use it
in large groups as a
background plant or
trim it and use it as a
midground plant in
large or small groups.*

Plants featured in the plant selection section

Species name	Common name	Type	Page
Alternanthera reineckii	Red hygrophila, copperleaf	BG	52
Anubias barteri var. nana	Dwarf anubias	SU	70
Anubias barteri	Broadleaf anubias	B/MG	60
Aponogeton boivinianus		SU	70
Aponogeton crispus	Wavy-edged swordplant	SU	70
Aponogeton madagascariensis	Madagascan laceplant	SU	71
Bacopa caroliniana	Giant bacopa	B/MG	60
Bolbitis heudelotii	Congo, or African, fern	SU	71
Cabomba caroliniana	Green cabomba	BG	52
Cabomba piauhyensis	Red cabomba	BG	53
Cardamine lyrata	Japanese cress	B/MG	61
Ceratophyllum demersum	Hornwort	FL	68
Ceratopteris thalictroides	Indian fern	FL	68
Crinum thaianum	Onion plant	BG	53
Cryptocoryne balansae		BG	53
Cryptocoryne beckettii		FG	64
Cryptocoryne undulata		FG	65
Cryptocoryne wendtii		FG	65
Cryptocoryne willisii		FG	65
Didiplis diandra	Water hedge	B/MG	61
Echinodorus bleheri	Broadleaf Amazon swordplant	BG	54
Echinodorus cordifolius	Radicans swordplant	SU	72
Echinodorus major	Ruffled Amazon swordplant	BG	54
Echinodorus tenellus	Pygmy chain swordplant	FG	66
Egeria densa	Pondweed, elodea	BG	54

Species name	Common name	Type	Page
Eleocharis acicularis	Hairgrass	FG	66
Eusteralis stellata	Star rotala	BG	55
Gymnocoronis spilanthoides	Spadeleaf plant	BG	55
Hemigraphis colorata	Crimson ivy	NA	75
Heteranthera zosterifolia	Stargrass	B/MG	62
Hydrocotyle leucocephala	Water pennywort	B/MG	62
Hygrophila difformis	Water wisteria	BG	55
Hygrophila polysperma	Dwarf hygrophila	BG	56
Lilaeopsis novae zelandiae	New Zealand grassplant	FG	66
Limnophila aquatica	Giant ambulia	BG	57
Ludwigia palustris	Green ludwigia	B/MG	63
Lysimachia nummularia 'Aurea'	Creeping Jenny, moneywort	B/MG	63
Microsorium pteropus	Java fern	SU	72
Myriophyllum hippuroides	Green myriophyllum, water milfoil	BG	57
Myriophyllum mattogrossense	Red myriophyllum, red milfoil	BG	57
Nuphar japonica	Japanese spatterdock	SU	73
Nymphaea lotus var. rubra	Red tiger lotus	SU	74
Ophiopogon japonicum var. giganteum		NA	75
Pistia stratiotes	Water lettuce	FL	68
Riccia fluitans	Crystalwort	FL	69
Rotala indica	Dwarf rotala	BG	58
Rotala macrandra	Giant red rotala	BG	58
Sagittaria platyphylla	Giant sagittaria	FG	67
Salvinia auriculata		FL	69
Vallisneria asiatica	Corkscrew vallisneria	BG	59
Vallisneria spiralis	Straight vallisneria	BG	59
Vesicularia dubyana	Java moss	SU	74

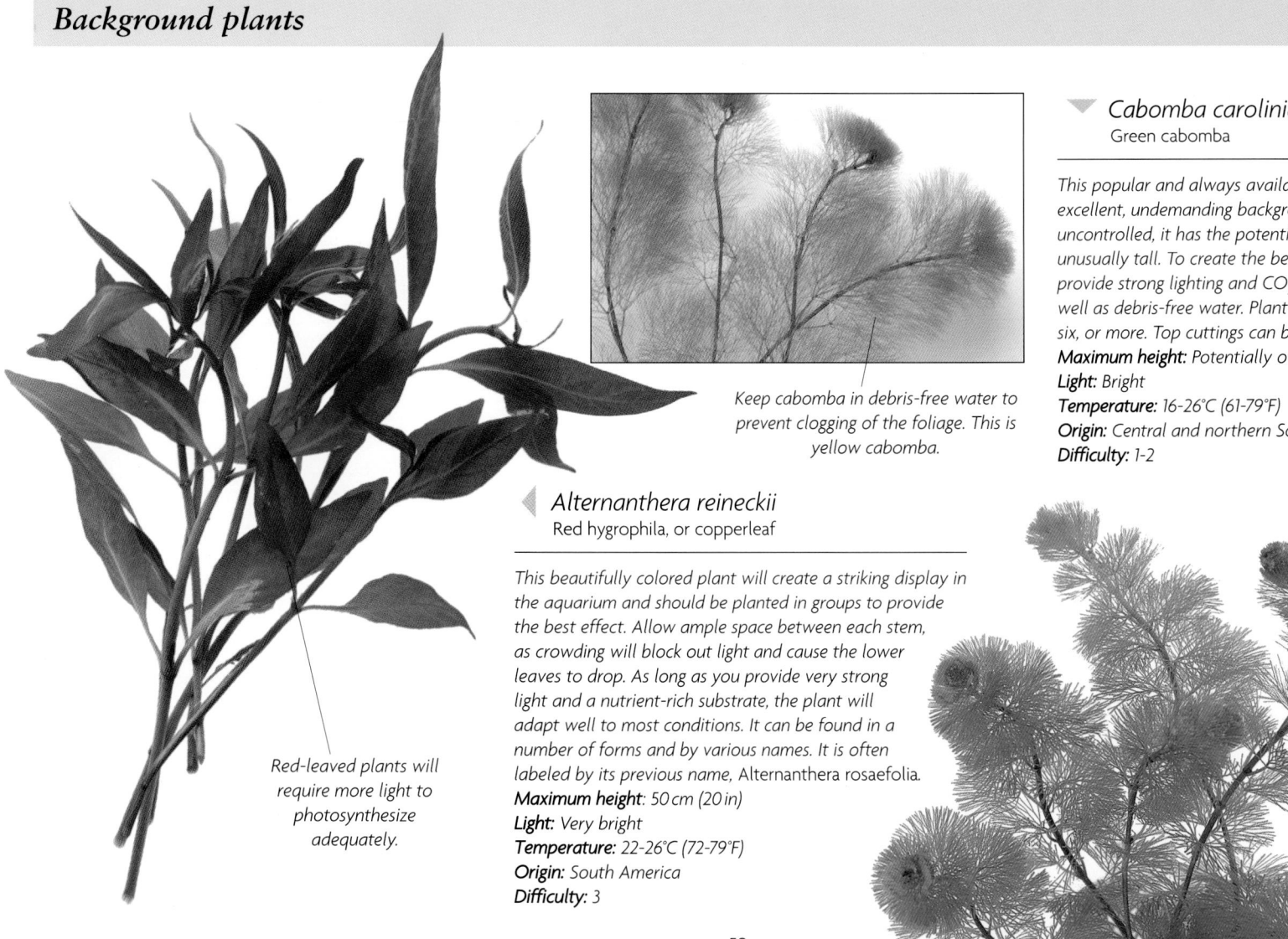

Keep cabomba in debris-free water to prevent clogging of the foliage. This is yellow cabomba.

Red-leaved plants will require more light to photosynthesize adequately.

▼ Cabomba caroliniana
Green cabomba

This popular and always available species is an excellent, undemanding background plant. If left uncontrolled, it has the potential to grow unusually tall. To create the best conditions, provide strong lighting and CO_2 fertilization, as well as debris-free water. Plant in groups of five, six, or more. Top cuttings can be replanted.

Maximum height: Potentially over 1.5 m (5 ft)
Light: Bright
Temperature: 16-26°C (61-79°F)
Origin: Central and northern South America
Difficulty: 1-2

◀ Alternanthera reineckii
Red hygrophila, or copperleaf

This beautifully colored plant will create a striking display in the aquarium and should be planted in groups to provide the best effect. Allow ample space between each stem, as crowding will block out light and cause the lower leaves to drop. As long as you provide very strong light and a nutrient-rich substrate, the plant will adapt well to most conditions. It can be found in a number of forms and by various names. It is often labeled by its previous name, Alternanthera rosaefolia.

Maximum height: 50 cm (20 in)
Light: Very bright
Temperature: 22-26°C (72-79°F)
Origin: South America
Difficulty: 3

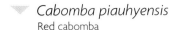

Cabomba piauhyensis
Red cabomba

If this plant is well cared for, it will look stunning in the aquarium, but it may prove a difficult species to keep happy. Strong lighting, soft water, and a good-quality, iron-rich fertilizer are essential, along with clean and clear water and additional CO_2.
Maximum height: *50 cm (20 in) or more*
Light: *Very bright*
Temperature: *24-28°C (75-82°F)*
Origin: *South and Central America*
Difficulty: *3-4*

The long, thick leaves of the onion plant are slow growing and hence prone to algae growth.

Crinum thaianum
Onion plant

A slow-growing plant, with thick, leathery leaves that will grow up to and along the water surface. The onion plant is tough and easy to maintain and can be kept in a tank with boisterous cichlids.
Maximum height: *1.5 m (5 ft)*
Light: *Moderate*
Temperature: *18-27°C (64-80°F)*
Origin: *Southeast Asia, mainly Thailand*
Difficulty: *1*

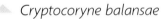

Cryptocoryne balansae

The long, thin leaves of this cryptocoryne are highly indented, giving it an attractive wrinkled appearance. The plant is undemanding and will tolerate hard water well. Although it will do well with less light, the growth rate and successful propagation are determined by the amount of light available. Once established and given good lighting, the plant should grow quickly and frequently produces new plants from runners. Plant it in groups toward the back and sides of the aquarium.
Maximum height: *30-45 cm (12-18 in)*
Light: *Moderate to bright*
Temperature: *23-28°C (73-82°F)*
Origin: *Thailand, Vietnam*
Difficulty: *2-3*

▶ ## Echinodorus bleheri
Broadleaf Amazon swordplant

The broadleaf sword is one of the most available and popular aquarium plants, similar in appearance to the almost equally popular Echinodorus amazonicus (Amazon swordplant). Use it in deep or large aquariums, either as a background plant in very well-spaced groups of two to four plants or as a single specimen plant. Provide iron and trim the roots before planting.
Maximum height: *50-60 cm (20-24 in)*
Light: *Moderate to bright*
Temperature: *22-28°C (72-82°F)*
Origin: *South America*
Difficulty: *1*

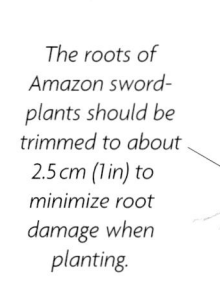

The roots of Amazon swordplants should be trimmed to about 2.5 cm (1 in) to minimize root damage when planting.

▼ ## Echinodorus major
Ruffled Amazon swordplant

An excellent, easy-to-keep background plant. It needs plenty of space, because once established, a single specimen may support more than 20 imposing leaves. As with many of the larger Amazon swordplants, it requires a constant and available source of iron to remain in good health.
Maximum height: *50-60 cm (20-24 in)*
Light: *Bright*
Temperature: *22-28°C (72-82°F)*
Origin: *Brazil*
Difficulty: *1*

▲ ## Egeria densa
Pondweed, elodea

Egeria densa is arguably the best-known aquarium plant, mainly because it is adaptable and easy to keep in a wide range of conditions. There are a number of forms available and it is known by several common names, although it is most commonly referred to as elodea, from the previous scientific name, Elodea densa. The plant requires no particular substrate as it produces few roots and gains little from being planted, other than being anchored in place. Egeria densa does particularly well in hard water; if kept in softer water, provide plenty of light and nutrients. It is a good background plant from which cuttings can be readily taken. Suitable for cold water or tropical aquariums.
Maximum height: *50 cm (20 in) or more*
Light: *Bright*
Temperature: *Up to 26°C (79°F)*
Origin: *Introduced worldwide*
Difficulty: *1*

Gymnocoronis spilanthoides
Spadeleaf plant

The thick, fleshy appearance of this plant provides a subtle contrast to neighboring species. In a nutrient-rich substrate, this undemanding plant will grow quickly and, when planted in groups, produces an attractive bushy display. In the right conditions, individual plants may grow as much as 20 cm (8 in) or more in a week. Regular pruning will eventually slow down growth rates.
Maximum height: 60 cm (24 in)
Light: Bright
Temperature: 19-26°C (66-79°F)
Origin: South America
Difficulty: 1-2

Eusteralis stellata
Star rotala

Although demanding, the star rotala will become a stunning aquarium plant if given the correct care. The light green leaves have a strong red-lilac underside, more evident toward the top of the plant, which provides a gradient that contrasts well with greener plants. The plant requires an available supply of nutrients and CO_2, combined with strong lighting.
Maximum height: 30-40 cm (12-16 in)
Light: Very bright
Temperature: 22-28°C (72-82°F)
Origin: Asia and Australia
Difficulty: 3-4

Hygrophila difformis
Water wisteria

An undemanding plant that produces finely branched decorative leaves that set it apart from other species. In low temperatures, the leaves will become less branched. Water wisteria prefers a nutrient-rich substrate and a good source of iron. If the lighting is too weak, the lower leaves become thin and drop off.
Maximum height: 50 cm (20 in)
Light: Bright
Temperature: 23-28°C (73-82°F)
Origin: India, Thailand
Difficulty: 1-2

Background plants

Hygrophila polysperma
Dwarf hygrophila

This is one of the most common aquarium plants available, mainly because it is undemanding and adaptable and will thrive in a range of aquariums, including cold water ones. Plant it in well-spaced groups of four, five, or more at the back of the aquarium to produce a bushy effect. Individual plants will need regular pruning and cuttings measuring 12 cm (4.7 in) or more can be replanted in the substrate. The leaves of dwarf hygrophila seem to be a favorite food of many snails and plant-eating fish.

Maximum height: 50 cm (20 in)
Light: Bright
Temperature: 18-30°C (64-86°F)
Origin: India
Difficulty: 1

Potted plants like this hygrophila usually contain 3 or 4 separate groups of stems, which can be separated before planting.

Above: If kept in bright light and regularly trimmed, giant ambulia will make a stunning bushy background plant. For best effect, plant groups of five or more, leaving about 5 cm (2 in) or more between each stem.

Limnophila aquatica
Giant ambulia

Although it is a common species of ambulia, this attractive plant can be quite demanding in the aquarium. To create optimum conditions, provide an iron-rich substrate or fertilizer, combined with bright light and soft water. The space between leaf nodes is dictated by the amount of light; in bright light, the space is shorter and the plant has a more attractive, bushy appearance.
Maximum height: 50 cm (20 in)
Light: Bright
Temperature: 22-27°C (72-80°F)
Origin: Southeast Asia, India
Difficulty: 3

Myriophyllum hippuroides
Green myriophyllum, water milfoil

If kept in groups of five, six, or more, this plant will create an attractive bushy effect. It must be kept in clean, clear water to prevent the fine, delicate leaves from becoming clogged. If the plant is regularly cut back, it will retain its bushy appearance; otherwise it will become thin.
Maximum height: 50 cm (20 in)
Light: Bright
Temperature: 15-25°C (59-77°F)
Origin: North and Central America
Difficulty: 2

Myriophyllum mattogrossense
Red myriophyllum, red milfoil

Ideally, arrange this beautiful rust-colored, feathery plant in small groups at the rear of the aquarium. Leave space between the plants to reduce light blockage. To appreciate the full color intensity of the plant, provide very strong lighting and frequent applications of iron-rich fertilizer. Make sure that the water is clean and free from debris and algae.
Maximum height: 60 cm (24 in)
Light: Very bright
Temperature: 22-28°C (72-82°F)
Origin: South America
Difficulty: 3

Red myriophyllum thrives on continual, steady fertilization in the aquarium.

Plants that are bunched like this should be separated before planting, or light will not reach the lower leaves and they will die off.

57

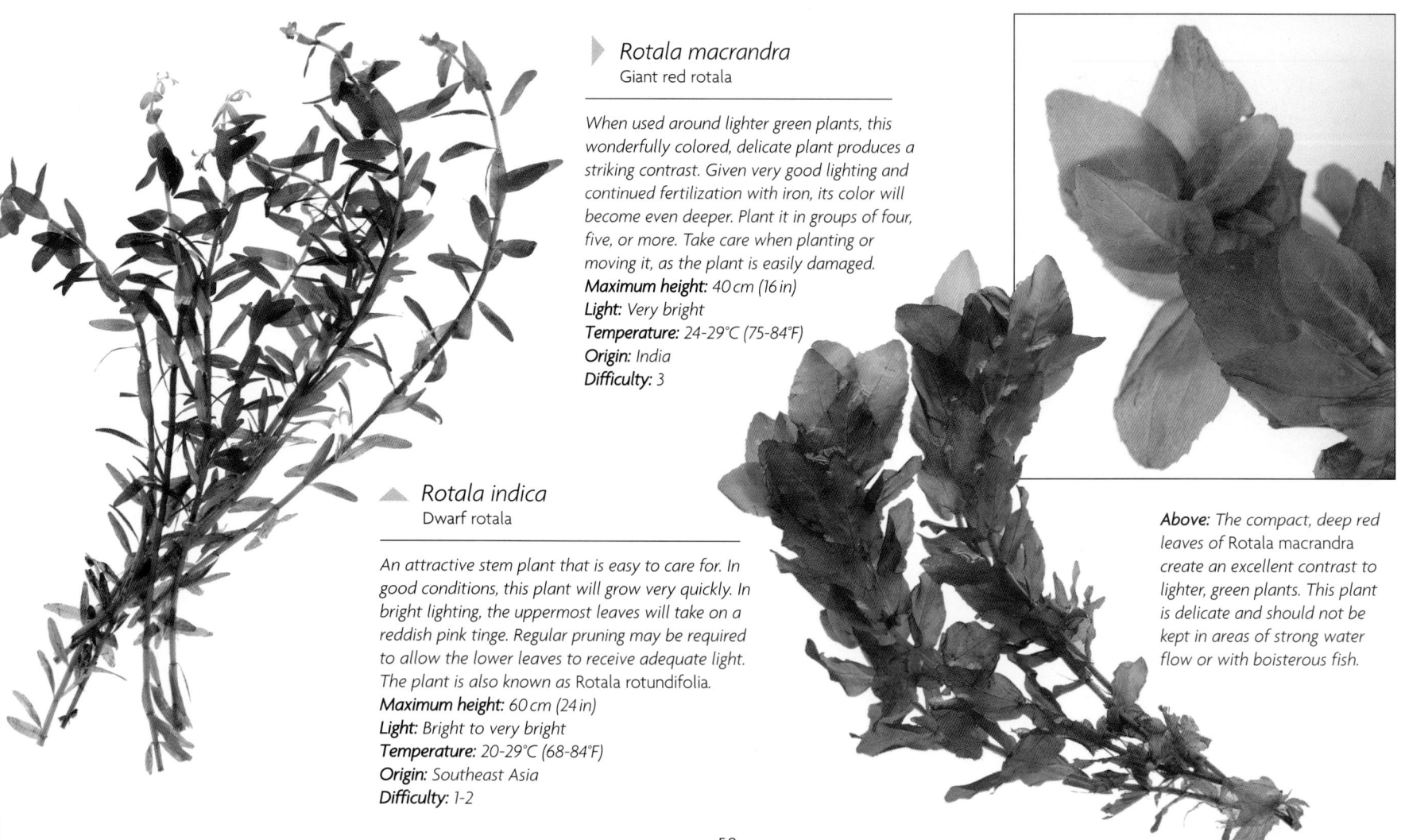

▶ Rotala macrandra
Giant red rotala

When used around lighter green plants, this wonderfully colored, delicate plant produces a striking contrast. Given very good lighting and continued fertilization with iron, its color will become even deeper. Plant it in groups of four, five, or more. Take care when planting or moving it, as the plant is easily damaged.
Maximum height: 40 cm (16 in)
Light: Very bright
Temperature: 24-29°C (75-84°F)
Origin: India
Difficulty: 3

▲ Rotala indica
Dwarf rotala

An attractive stem plant that is easy to care for. In good conditions, this plant will grow very quickly. In bright lighting, the uppermost leaves will take on a reddish pink tinge. Regular pruning may be required to allow the lower leaves to receive adequate light. The plant is also known as Rotala rotundifolia.
Maximum height: 60 cm (24 in)
Light: Bright to very bright
Temperature: 20-29°C (68-84°F)
Origin: Southeast Asia
Difficulty: 1-2

Above: The compact, deep red leaves of Rotala macrandra create an excellent contrast to lighter, green plants. This plant is delicate and should not be kept in areas of strong water flow or with boisterous fish.

Vallisneria spiralis
Straight vallisneria

This tough, undemanding plant has been a popular addition to aquariums for many years. Once established, it will produce many daughter plants from runners, and in good conditions, will need to be thinned regularly. The plant does better in strong light, but will tolerate subdued conditions. Plant it in groups around the back and sides of the aquarium.
Maximum height: 40-50 cm (16-20 in)
Light: Bright
Temperature: 15-30°C (59-86°F)
Origin: Widespread in the tropics and subtropics
Difficulty: 1

Right: Straight vallisneria is one of the best-known and most popular aquatic plants available. In this specimen, flowers can be seen on long, spiraled stems.

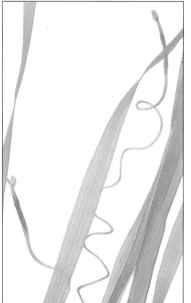

Vallisneria asiatica
Corkscrew vallisneria

The corkscrew vallisneria is an attractive, undemanding plant that should thrive in most aquariums. It may not appreciate water that is too soft and needs ample light. A smaller plant, Vallisneria tortifolia, is ideal for the middle foreground of the aquarium.
Maximum height: 30-40 cm (12-16 in)
Light: Bright
Temperature: 24-28°C (75-82°F)
Origin: Japan
Difficulty: 1-2

The thick, tough leaves of the broadleaf anubias can be grown out of water.

◀ Anubias barteri
Broadleaf anubias

A number of species are collectively grouped (spec. barteri) as broadleaf anubias, but there is little difference between them. The plant is relatively slow growing and produces tough, firm, dark leaves, which makes it ideal for an aquarium with plant-destructive fish, such as cichlids or herbivorous species. Use the plant singly in the midground or arrange a group in the background. They appreciate a warm substrate and additional CO_2.

Maximum height: 15-33 cm (6-13 in)
Light: Moderate to bright
Temperature: 22-28°C (72-82°F)
Origin: West Africa
Difficulty: 2

▶ Bacopa caroliniana
Giant bacopa

A fast-growing, interestingly shaped plant that will do well in most aquariums, providing sufficient light and nutrients are available. In very bright light, the leaves often exhibit a slight red-bronze color. If provided with adequate CO_2 the plant will do well in harder water. Best arranged in groups of four, five, or more plants along the back, middle, or sides of the aquarium.

Maximum height: 30-40 cm (12-16 in)
Light: Bright
Temperature: 20-28°C (68-82°F)
Origin: Southern and Central United States
Difficulty: 2

Bacopa caroliniana is an attractive plant that can be used in harder water.

Cardamine lyrata
Japanese cress

An unusual plant with an attractively "messy"
appearance. It is sensitive to chemicals and
warmer water, although it will tolerate higher
temperatures for short periods. Apart from
needing good lighting, the plant is highly
adaptable in a stable environment. Ideally,
plant it in groups in the center of the
aquarium against a dark background,
such as a piece of bogwood.
Maximum height: 40 cm (16 in)
Light: Bright to very bright
Temperature: 16-22°C (61-72°F)
Origin: China, Japan, Korea
Difficulty: 2

Above: Mixing tall, fine-leaved, bushy
plants such as Didiplis diandra *with
smaller, broad-leaved plants creates
an attractive display in the aquarium.*

Didiplis diandra
Water hedge

When planted in groups of ten or more individual stems,
the "pine needle" leaves create an attractive foliage
appearance. Do not place individual plants too close
together, as the plant may produce a number of offshoots,
thickening the group. In bright light, the tips of the plant
will turn a pleasing reddish color. The plant appreciates the
addition of an iron-rich fertilizer.
Maximum height: 20-33 cm (8-13 in)
Light: Very bright
Temperature: 20-26°C (68-79°F)
Origin: North America
Difficulty: 2-3

▼ Heteranthera zosterifolia
Stargrass

Although this plant can reach up to 50 cm (20 in) in length, it can be regularly trimmed without any ill effects. If kept relatively short, plants can be grouped to create an attractive bushy appearance graded from the rear of the aquarium toward the midground. Apart from requiring regular applications of fertilizer and a good light source, the plant is relatively undemanding.
Maximum height: 40-50 cm (16-20 in)
Light: Bright
Temperature: 22-26°C (72-79°F)
Origin: South America
Difficulty: 2

Above: Bushy clumps of Heteranthera zosterifolia are ideal for providing interest in the midground and background areas of an aquarium display. Simply trim the stems to different lengths.

If this plant is allowed to reach the surface, it will produce many sideshoots covering the water surface.

There are a number of color types of this plant available, including one with an attractive red coloration on the underside of the leaves.

▲ Hydrocotyle leucocephala
Water pennywort, Brazilian pennywort

The leaf shape and thin stalk lend this plant an endearingly untidy appearance. If left unchecked it will soon reach the surface, where the leaves will spread and block out the light to other plants. Top cuttings can be taken, but the remaining stem is less likely to continue growing than is the case with most other stem plants.
Maximum height: 50 cm (20 in)
Light: Bright
Temperature: 20-28°C (68-82°F)
Origin: Brazil
Difficulty: 1-2

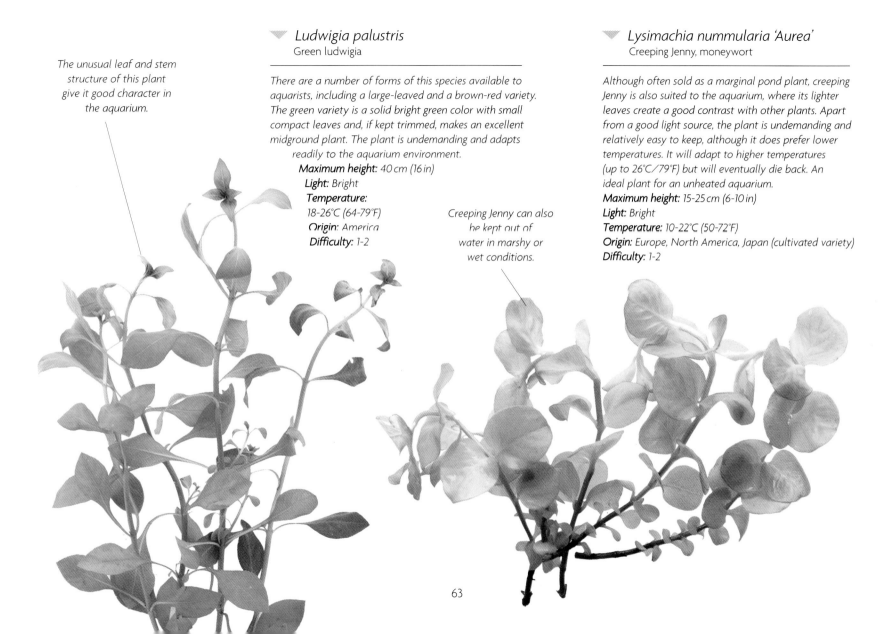

The unusual leaf and stem structure of this plant give it good character in the aquarium.

▼ *Ludwigia palustris*
Green ludwigia

There are a number of forms of this species available to aquarists, including a large-leaved and a brown-red variety. The green variety is a solid bright green color with small compact leaves and, if kept trimmed, makes an excellent midground plant. The plant is undemanding and adapts readily to the aquarium environment.

Maximum height: *40 cm (16 in)*
Light: *Bright*
Temperature:
18-26°C (64-79°F)
Origin: *America*
Difficulty: *1-2*

Creeping Jenny can also be kept out of water in marshy or wet conditions.

▼ *Lysimachia nummularia 'Aurea'*
Creeping Jenny, moneywort

Although often sold as a marginal pond plant, creeping Jenny is also suited to the aquarium, where its lighter leaves create a good contrast with other plants. Apart from a good light source, the plant is undemanding and relatively easy to keep, although it does prefer lower temperatures. It will adapt to higher temperatures (up to 26°C/79°F) but will eventually die back. An ideal plant for an unheated aquarium.

Maximum height: *15-25 cm (6-10 in)*
Light: *Bright*
Temperature: *10-22°C (50-72°F)*
Origin: *Europe, North America, Japan (cultivated variety)*
Difficulty: *1-2*

Foreground plants

Right: Cryptocorynes make excellent foreground plants that will require little maintenance once established.

▲ Cryptocoryne beckettii

This plant is slow growing in the aquarium, but can be encouraged by providing a warm substrate (using a heating cable) and a good supply of nutrients; otherwise, it is undemanding. Plant it in groups toward the aquarium foreground.

Maximum height: 15-20 cm (6-8 in)

Light: Undemanding

Temperature: 24-28°C (75-82°F)

Origin: Sri Lanka

Difficulty: 1-2

The small leaves and crowded stems of this plant make good hiding places for small, bottom-dwelling fish.

Cryptocoryne undulata
Undulate cryptocoryne

Once established, the undulate cryptocoryne is an excellent foreground plant that reproduces readily in the aquarium and is easy to keep. In strong lighting the leaves keep their brown-red color; otherwise, they will turn green. The plant does not appreciate significant short-term changes in water quality.

Maximum height: 10-20 cm (4-8 in)
Light: Undemanding
Temperature: 22-28°C (72-82°F)
Origin: Sri Lanka
Difficulty: 1

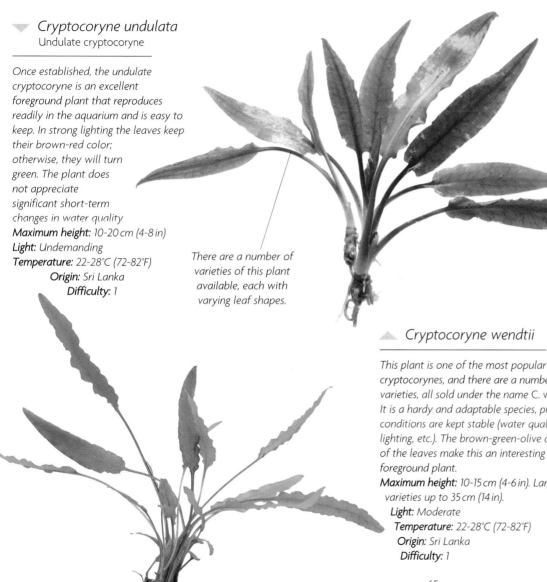

There are a number of varieties of this plant available, each with varying leaf shapes.

Cryptocoryne willisii

This plant makes a good foreground plant, either singly or in groups. The leaves have a leathery appearance due to the plant's amphibious nature. In brighter light the plant will form a compact group of leaves that should spread along the substrate. This cryptocoryne is hardier than many similar species and appreciates a buildup of debris around the base. Also labeled as Cryptocoryne nevellii.

Maximum height: 15 cm (6 in)
Light: Bright to moderate
Temperature: 19-28°C (66-82°F)
Origin: Sri Lanka
Difficulty: 1-2

Cryptocoryne wendtii

This plant is one of the most popular cryptocorynes, and there are a number of varieties, all sold under the name C. wendtii. It is a hardy and adaptable species, providing conditions are kept stable (water quality, lighting, etc.). The brown-green-olive colors of the leaves make this an interesting foreground plant.

Maximum height: 10-15 cm (4-6 in). Larger varieties up to 35 cm (14 in).
Light: Moderate
Temperature: 22-28°C (72-82°F)
Origin: Sri Lanka
Difficulty: 1

Foreground plants

Echinodorus tenellus
Pygmy chain swordplant

Once established, this excellent foreground plant will spread prolifically, creating a lawnlike appearance. Although this species does not do well in harder water, there are varieties that may do better, such as E. tenellus var. parvulus. When planting, allow adequate space for spreading.
Maximum height: 7.5-13 cm (3-5 in)
Light: Bright
Temperature: 17-27°C (62-80°F)
Origin: Areas of North and South America
Difficulty: 2

Eleocharis acicularis
Hairgrass

This grasslike plant will form a dense carpet of vegetation across the aquarium floor, which is especially appreciated by smaller fish. Keep the aquarium water as free from debris as possible so that the fine strands do not become clogged. As long as it has sufficient light, the plant is undemanding. A slightly smaller, but less common, dwarf variety (Eleocharis parvulus) is also available.
Maximum height: 25 cm (10 in), but usually 10-15 cm (4-6 in)
Light: Bright to very bright
Temperature: 10-25°C (50-77°F)
Origin: Worldwide (tropics)
Difficulty: 2-3

Hairgrass can become quickly clogged with debris. To reduce buildup, gently disturb the plant regularly by wafting water through the leaves.

Lilaeopsis novae zelandiae
New Zealand grassplant

This excellent foreground plant will create a dense matting of vegetation across the substrate floor. Strong lighting is required to keep it in the best of health and, provided this is supplied, it will adapt to a range of water conditions and temperatures. This plant has both an aquatic and a terrestrial form and can easily be grown out of water. It is often confused with, and sold as, Echinodorus tenellus.
Maximum height: 7.5-13 cm (3-5 in)
Light: Very bright
Temperature: 18-28°C (64-82°F)
Origin: New Zealand
Difficulty: 2

Once established, this plant should spread along the foreground.

Sagittaria platyphylla *has thick leaves and a solid appearance that differentiates it from other foreground species. Many smaller fish will appreciate the hiding places that it provides.*

▼ ## Sagittaria platyphylla
Giant sagittaria

This unusual little plant has thick, 1-cm (0.4-in)-wide leaves that will spread out in an umbrella fashion along the foreground. The plant can be used singly in open spaces, as a middle-ground plant or grouped toward the center of the aquarium. Provide plenty of light. Suitable for a cold water aquarium.

Maximum height: *20 cm (8 in)*
Light: *Very bright*
Temperature: *16-26°C (61-79°F)*
Origin: *North America (Mississippi)*
Difficulty: *2*

The robust leaves of this plant mean it can be kept in areas of medium-strong water flow.

Floating plants

▼ Ceratophyllum demersum
Hornwort

Although hornwort is often planted in the substrate, it is really a floating species. It does not produce roots when planted, so derives no benefit from being "underground." Hornwort is also very brittle and breaks up easily. As a floating plant this is not such a problem, as it is a method of propagation; any pieces that break off will become new plants. Hornwort is particularly well suited to colder aquariums and, apart from debris-free water and good lighting, makes no special demands.
Maximum height: 40 cm (16 in)
Light: Bright
Temperature: 10-28°C (50-82°F)
Origin: Worldwide
Difficulty: 2

▲ Ceratopteris thalictroides
Indian fern

This plant is mostly sold as an upright submerged plant for substrate planting, but does slightly better as a floating plant, requiring less light and growing more quickly. Given adequate fertilization, this plant is very easy to grow and an excellent floating species. If it is used as a substrate-planted specimen, plant it singly and make sure that the top of the roots is just above the substrate surface.
Maximum height: 35 cm (14 in)
Light: Bright
Temperature: 22-26°C (72-79°F)
Origin: America, Africa, Asia, northern Australia
Difficulty: 1

▼ Pistia stratiotes
Water lettuce

Surface-dwelling fish will find good hiding places among the trailing roots of this attractive floating plant. Provide space and ventilation between the water surface and the lights to prevent the leaves from being burned. This undemanding plant will spread rapidly, producing many small plants.
Maximum size: Usually 5-6 cm (2-2.4 in), but may reach 10 cm (4 in) wide
Light: Bright
Temperature: 23-28°C (73-82°F)
Origin: Tropical regions
Difficulty: 1-2

Below: The many small protective hairs on the upper leaf surface of Salvinia auriculata *help this small plant to repel water and remain above the water surface.*

 Riccia fluitans
Crystalwort

This tiny plant divides rapidly, forming a tangled mat of attractive floating leaves. Avoid surface water movement; otherwise, the plant will simply be blown around the aquarium. Apart from good-quality, nutrient-rich water, the plant has no special requirements and will adapt to a wide range of temperatures and conditions.
Light: *Moderate*
Temperature: *15-30°C (59-86°F)*
Origin: *Worldwide*
Difficulty: *1-2*

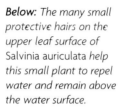

▲ Salvinia auriculata

Other than adequate ventilation to prevent scorching, this small floating plant has no special requirements. It will provide good cover and areas of shade for smaller fish.
Light: *Moderate*
Temperature: *21-25°C (70-77°F)*
Origin: *South and Central America*
Difficulty: *1-2*

Specimen or unusual plants

▼ Anubias barteri var. nana
Dwarf anubias

The dwarf anubias can be used as an attractive foreground plant, but may be put to better use attached to bogwood or rocks higher up in the aquarium. It is undemanding and will quite happily grow in low-light conditions. Although slow growing, it makes a welcome addition to the aquarium once it has spread over bogwood. It can also be grown emerging from the water surface.

Maximum height: 7.5-13 cm (3-5 in)
Light: Undemanding
Temperature: 22-28°C (72-82°F)
Origin: West Africa, Cameroon
Difficulty: 2

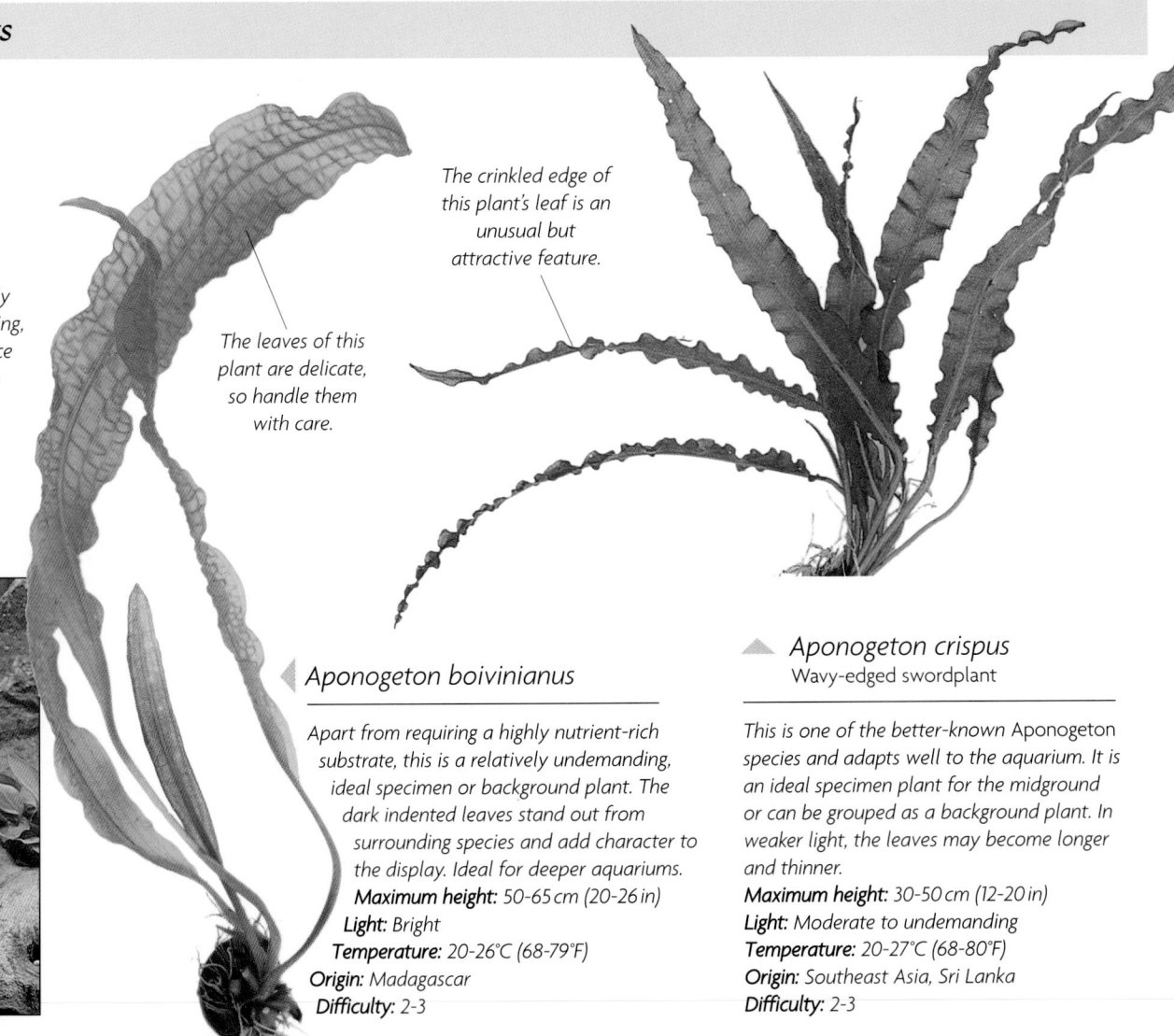

The crinkled edge of this plant's leaf is an unusual but attractive feature.

The leaves of this plant are delicate, so handle them with care.

◄ Aponogeton boivinianus

Apart from requiring a highly nutrient-rich substrate, this is a relatively undemanding, ideal specimen or background plant. The dark indented leaves stand out from surrounding species and add character to the display. Ideal for deeper aquariums.

Maximum height: 50-65 cm (20-26 in)
Light: Bright
Temperature: 20-26°C (68-79°F)
Origin: Madagascar
Difficulty: 2-3

▲ Aponogeton crispus
Wavy-edged swordplant

This is one of the better-known Aponogeton species and adapts well to the aquarium. It is an ideal specimen plant for the midground or can be grouped as a background plant. In weaker light, the leaves may become longer and thinner.

Maximum height: 30-50 cm (12-20 in)
Light: Moderate to undemanding
Temperature: 20-27°C (68-80°F)
Origin: Southeast Asia, Sri Lanka
Difficulty: 2-3

Aponogeton madagascariensis
Madagascan laceplant

This highly unusual and interesting plant has little leaf tissue, sporting instead a leaf structure of veins. To grow it successfully, it is important to provide the correct conditions. The water must be clear, soft, and free of debris. Algae will quickly kill the plant. It prefers a shaded position and cooler water. It is quite common for this plant to grow strong and healthily at first, with no apparent problems, only to start to die later.

Maximum height: 25-40 cm (10-16 in)
Light: Moderate or restricted
Temperature: 20-24°C (68-75°F)
Origin: Madagascar
Difficulty: 4

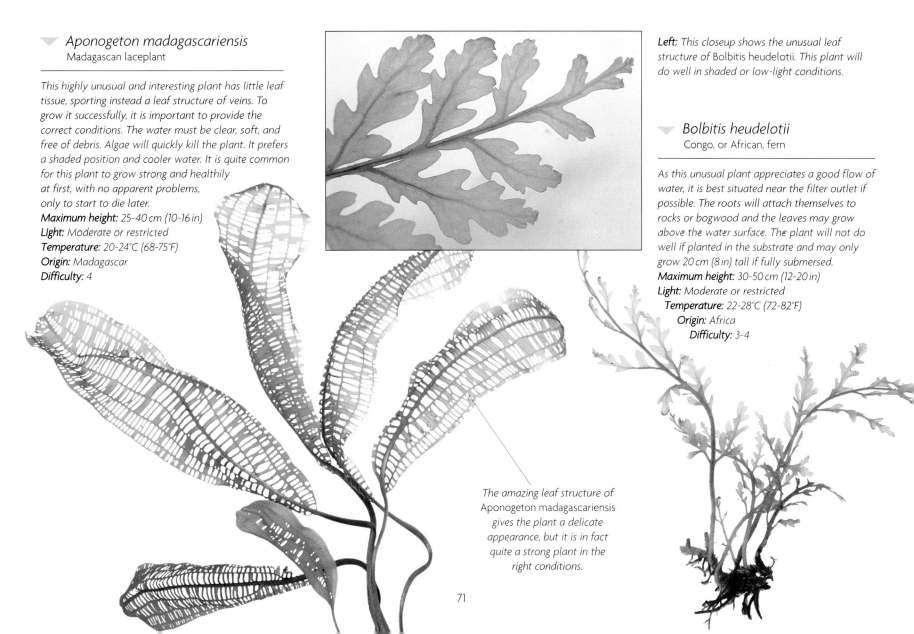

Left: This closeup shows the unusual leaf structure of Bolbitis heudelotii. This plant will do well in shaded or low-light conditions.

Bolbitis heudelotii
Congo, or African, fern

As this unusual plant appreciates a good flow of water, it is best situated near the filter outlet if possible. The roots will attach themselves to rocks or bogwood and the leaves may grow above the water surface. The plant will not do well if planted in the substrate and may only grow 20 cm (8 in) tall if fully submersed.

Maximum height: 30-50 cm (12-20 in)
Light: Moderate or restricted
Temperature: 22-28°C (72-82°F)
Origin: Africa
Difficulty: 3-4

The amazing leaf structure of Aponogeton madagascariensis gives the plant a delicate appearance, but it is in fact quite a strong plant in the right conditions.

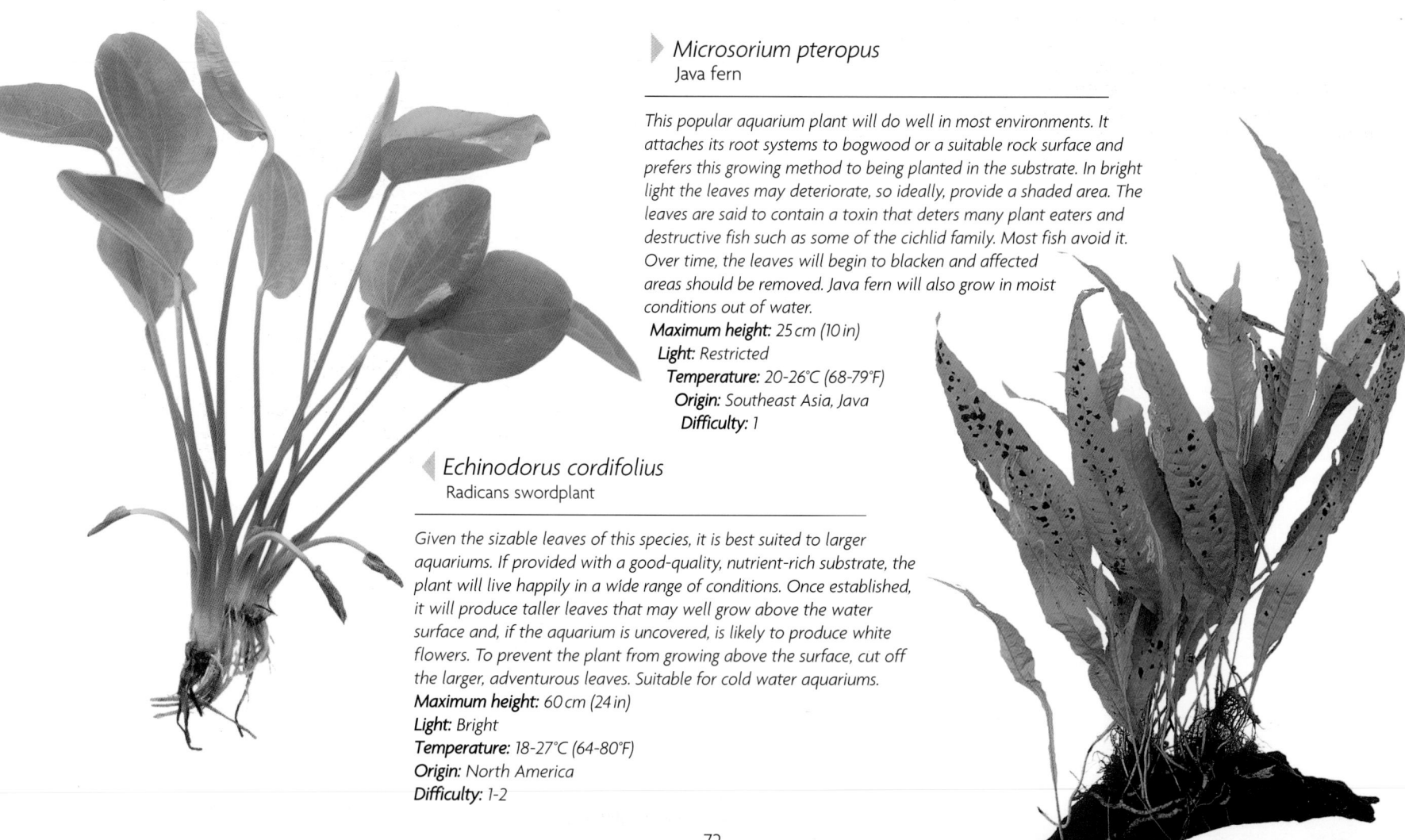

▶ Microsorium pteropus
Java fern

This popular aquarium plant will do well in most environments. It attaches its root systems to bogwood or a suitable rock surface and prefers this growing method to being planted in the substrate. In bright light the leaves may deteriorate, so ideally, provide a shaded area. The leaves are said to contain a toxin that deters many plant eaters and destructive fish such as some of the cichlid family. Most fish avoid it. Over time, the leaves will begin to blacken and affected areas should be removed. Java fern will also grow in moist conditions out of water.

Maximum height: 25 cm (10 in)
Light: Restricted
Temperature: 20-26°C (68-79°F)
Origin: Southeast Asia, Java
Difficulty: 1

◀ Echinodorus cordifolius
Radicans swordplant

Given the sizable leaves of this species, it is best suited to larger aquariums. If provided with a good-quality, nutrient-rich substrate, the plant will live happily in a wide range of conditions. Once established, it will produce taller leaves that may well grow above the water surface and, if the aquarium is uncovered, is likely to produce white flowers. To prevent the plant from growing above the surface, cut off the larger, adventurous leaves. Suitable for cold water aquariums.

Maximum height: 60 cm (24 in)
Light: Bright
Temperature: 18-27°C (64-80°F)
Origin: North America
Difficulty: 1-2

Below: *A number of varieties of* Echinodorus cordifolius *are available, each with slightly different leaf shapes. The plant is a dominating midground or background plant.*

The crinkled, light green leaves of Nuphar japonica should be given space in the aquarium.

Nuphar japonica
Japanese spatterdock

Given adequate lighting and a good substrate, this plant should do well in most aquariums. The attractive large leaves mean that it is seen to best effect in its own space in the aquarium. The plant will live happily in an unheated aquarium and makes an interesting cold water species.
Maximum height: *60 cm (24 in)*
Light: *Bright to very bright*
Temperature: *12-25°C (54-77°F)*
Origin: *Japan*
Difficulty: *2-3*

Specimen or unusual plants

▶ *Nymphaea lotus var. rubra*
Red tiger lotus

A green form of this plant (N. lotus var.
viridis) is also available, but various
hybrids and color forms of the two are
more commonly seen than pure strains. This
is a stunning and dominating plant that needs
ample room. To ensure that it remains a
compact, manageable specimen in the average
aquarium, remove any leaves that reach the
surface. However, in the larger aquarium,
leaves on the surface will provide excellent
shading and cover for surface swimmers.
Maximum height: 30-50 cm (12-20 in)
Light: Bright
Temperature: 22-28°C (72-82°F)
Origin: Africa
Difficulty: 2

▶ *Vesicularia dubyana*
Java moss

This undemanding moss makes an excellent addition to
the aquarium, where it can be used to cover rocks or
bogwood. If attached to an object, it will establish
quickly and slowly spread. Prune and trim it regularly to
retain the desired shape and spread pattern. The moss is
often best used combined with Java fern.
Light: Undemanding
Temperature: 20-30°C (68-86°F)
Origin: Southeast Asia, Malaysia, Java, India
Difficulty: 1

Below: Java moss is a versatile
aquarium plant with many uses. It
can be attached to rock, wood, or
around the base of other plants.

Nonaquatic plants

Hemigraphis colorata
Crimson ivy

The highly indented leaves and intense, almost metallic, color of this plant make it an unusual specimen for the aquarium. The topside of the leaves is dark green, while the underside sports an intense purple-red color. This plant can survive well underwater for 10 months or more.

Maximum height: 20 cm (8 in)
Light: Bright
Temperature: 22-28°C (72-82°F)
Origin: Possibly Indonesia
Difficulty: 3

Right: The thick, inflexible roots of Ophiopogon japonicum var. giganteum are an indication of its terrestrial nature. In its natural environment it is exposed to floods that may last for many months, giving it an ability to survive underwater.

Ophiopogon japonicum var. giganteum

This unusual-looking plant may look slightly out of place in a fully planted aquarium, but does have a distinctive appearance that demands attention. The common name of fountain plant is used in the aquarium trade, whereas mondo grass describes it in terrestrial gardening. The species requires little light and may survive for up to 12 months underwater.

Maximum height: 35 cm (14 in)
Light: Undemanding
Temperature: 18-26°C (64-79°F)
Origin: Possibly China, Japan, Korea
Difficulty: 3

75

INDEX

Page numbers in **bold** indicate major entries; *italics* refer to captions and annotations; plain type indicates other text entries.

CREDITS

Practical photographs by Geoffrey Rogers © Interpet Publishing.

The publishers would like to thank the following photographers
for providing images, credited here by page number and
position: B(Bottom), T(Top), C(Center), BL(Bottom Left), etc.

Aqua Press (M-P & C Piednoir): Title page, copyright page, 11(BR),
12(T, B), 14(R), 26, 29(R), 34(BL), 42, 43, 47(T), 48, 49(TC), 64(R), 67(L),
73(L)
Mike Sandford: 45(TL), 49(TR, B)
W A Tomey: 30, 56(R), 61(C)

Illustrations by Phil Holmes and Stuart Watkinson © Interpet
Publishing.

The publishers would like to thank The Water Zoo, Peterborough
for providing facilities for practical photography. Thanks are also
due to Anglo Aquarium Ltd., Enfield, Middx; Dutch Aquarium
Supplies, Ooltgensplaat, The Netherlands; Green Line Aquatic
Plants, Spalding, Lincs; Heaver Tropics, Ash, Kent.